KT-481-375

Introduction
By Professor Robert Winston

Expectant mothers have little practical experience in modern society. In the past, women spent many formative years learning about pregnancy, birth and babies. The skills of motherhood were absorbed by osmosis from their mothers, grandmothers, aunts, older sisters, and cousins. Extended families living in close proximity are largely a thing of the past in the UK. Now parents have been at school longer, have often been students or worked full-time and gained important skills, but they've grown up without the experience of pregnancies, births and babies that families were once involved with at home.

As an obstetrician for many decades I have seen how pregnant woman today suddenly enter a medicalised realm of babies, scans, antenatal classes and birth plans. Pregnancy and birth are now bewildering and it can all seem very different to normal life. New parents can therefore be hit hard by the shock of being responsible for the growth and nurture of this small, fragile creature – their baby.

A study by The Essential Parent Company showed that around 80 percent of new parents felt anxious and lacked the practical skills they needed to prepare for their birth and look after their new baby. A third of UK parents had never seen a family member breastfeeding. Breastfeeding is a learned skill and without seeing it happening lots of new mums really struggle to know what to do, and usually leave hospital before their milk has come in and breastfeeding has been established. It is no wonder that although the vast majority of mothers in the UK want to breastfeed, we end up with one of the lowest levels of breastfeeding in Europe.

Fundamentally, human beings learn how to do things by seeing other people do them first. Other animals may be born with more instinctive abilities to care for their young, but we have to learn our birthing and parenting skills from others. Handing on these skills from mother to daughter helps us to look after our uniquely vulnerable babies. In modern Britain this highly evolved system of learning and passing on practical skills has been watered down, and pregnant women and new mums don't feel well equipped to give birth or look after their babies.

With *The Essential Pregnancy & Birth Guide* (www.essentialparent.com) we aim to help you, a prospective mum, understand what's going on as the pregnancy progresses, learn about how your body gives birth to your baby and to prepare you for all the practical skills you will need to nurture your baby when the exciting day of the birth finally arrives.

Chapter 1: Looking after yourself

Pregnancy is an incredibly exciting time, especially if it's your first baby. There is so much that is completely new – and so much to look forward to with the arrival of a brand-new member of your family. That said, the prospect of everything changing fills some people with wonder and others with anxiety. This chapter aims to go over some of the things you're likely to experience and how to make sure you look after yourself, for your own sake and for your baby's. Some of it is common sense: for example, eating a balanced healthy diet, and not smoking or drinking. But there are also some new facts you'll need to be aware of, such as foods to avoid. You may also experience new feelings about which you might welcome some advice. We also hope our practical guidance on issues ranging from buying clothes to fit the bump, to when to inform your workplace that you're pregnant, might help you avoid a few potential pitfalls along the way.

What should I eat when I am pregnant?

It's really important to make sure you eat a healthy and balanced diet throughout your pregnancy – for your own health as well as that of your unborn baby. Women used to think that they had to eat for two during their pregnancy, but this is not the case. In fact, you need to take in the same amount of calories that you would normally eat all the way through your pregnancy – until the last three months (third trimester). At this stage you should increase your intake by no more than 200 calories a day – which is the equivalent of a healthy snack: for example, two pieces of fruit.

How can I get a balanced diet?

Fruit and vegetables are incredibly important during pregnancy as they contain all the vitamins and minerals that your baby needs to grow. Make sure you should include a wide variety in your diet.

You need carbohydrates (rice, pasta or bread) for energy. You should aim for a small amount with every meal, but avoid those made with refined white flour or rice. Eat brown rice or wholemeal bread or pasta, they are digested more slowly and help with constipation that many women suffer during pregnancy.

Proteins are the building blocks of body tissue and are needed for structure, function, and regulation of the tissues and organs. You find them in meat, fish, eggs, nuts and pulses. Aim to eat protein foods twice a day and choose lean varieties where possible.

Dairy products (milk, cheese and yoghurt) provide the calcium that a baby needs for bone development. You should aim for about four servings of dairy products a day. If your diet does not contain enough calcium, your developing baby will actually take calcium from your bones. Full-fat milk contains the most calcium, but you can continue to drink the milk you usually drink as long as you make sure you are getting enough calcium in your diet.

When it comes to foods and drinks high in fats and sugars, they should be minimised or cut out completely. Not only do they contain lots of calories, which can contribute to weight gain, but they also do not contain many nutrients, and so will not help with your growing baby.

However, it is important to include good fats in your pregnancy diet because they contribute to brain and eye development in the fetus. In particular, omega 3 is incredibly important and found in oily fish as well as nuts and seeds (for example, walnuts and flaxseed oil). If you don't feel like you're getting enough omega 3 in your diet, you can take a supplement; however, choose one that doesn't have the word 'liver' in it, such as cod liver oil, as this can contain unhealthy levels of vitamin A.

Why do some people have food cravings?

Many women develop food cravings in pregnancy, and while sweet foods are the most common, all kinds of foods, from pickles to oranges, can be craved. Opinion is divided on whether these cravings have a function, although pica (craving eating strange non-foods like limescale and coal) has been associated with iron deficiency (even though these are not iron-rich foods).

Why do some women develop aversions to certain foods in pregnancy?

One reason is that pregnancy hormones make them very sensitive to smell and taste, which can put them off a variety of strong foods. Similarly some pregnant women go off caffeinated drinks and foods that are more likely to cause food poisoning. There is an evolutionary theory that this cautious diet may serve to protect the developing fetus, especially in the first trimester, from toxins and food-borne infections that can cross the placenta.

Can I get everything I need if I follow a vegetarian or vegan diet?

If you are a vegetarian you should be able to get plenty of protein such as lentils and beans. However, you will need to make sure you get plenty of omega 3 fatty acids – flaxseeds are a particularly good source. If you are a vegan or are on a strict 'fad' diet, speak to your doctor or a registered dietitian as you may be at risk of becoming deficient in vitamin B^{12} and you will need to take a supplement.

Which foods are important to avoid in pregnancy?

Sadly, there are many foods you should avoid during pregnancy. It can feel a bit overwhelming, especially if you are eating out, to know what you can safely eat and what you need to avoid. Friends may tell you that they ate everything they wanted and their baby was fine, but there are real risks to eating foods that may contain parasites or infections that can cross the placenta and make your baby ill, or in extreme cases, cause you to miscarry. To be on the safe side, it's really important to wash fresh fruit and vegetables before eating, and to make sure your food is stored properly and cooked thoroughly. Never eat foods that have passed their use-by date. Don't feel embarrassed about asking restaurants what is in their dishes.

Are meat and cheese safe to eat?

Avoid any raw or undercooked meat or meat products, and the same goes for eggs. Cold-cured meats such as salami should be thoroughly cooked before you eat them. This is because raw and undercooked meats and eggs may contain bacteria and parasites such as salmonella and toxoplasmosis (see page 10) that could harm your baby. Some cheeses should also be avoided. Soft cheeses (unpasteurised, mould-ripened or blue) can contain bacteria such as listeria (see page 10). Hard cheeses are safe to eat. Cheeses made with unpasteurised milk can be eaten if they have been cooked thoroughly first.

Why do I need to limit vitamin A?

While you need some vitamin A in your diet, too much (or too little) can affect your baby's development, which is why you also shouldn't take a vitamin supplement that contains vitamin A (see page 11). Foods such as liver and liver pâté contain excessively high levels of vitamin A and should be avoided. Vitamin A is a fat-soluble vitamin, which means it is stored in the liver and fat cells of the body. Safe vitamin A is available in two forms: beta-carotene (found in carrots, oranges and sweet potatoes), helps skin-cell production and immunity, and is converted into a safe form of vitamin A by the body; and retinol (essential for eye development) is found in safe levels in dairy products and eggs.

Is it safe to eat fish?

When it comes to seafood, shark, marlin and swordfish should be avoided and tuna should be limited to no more than two steaks or four cans a week. This is because as predatory fish, they store high levels of mercury in their muscles, which can be harmful to your developing baby's brain. You can have shellfish during your pregnancy if it has been cooked thoroughly. If you're going to eat sushi, make sure any raw fish has been frozen first.

ILLNESS CAUSED BY PARASITES AND BACTERIA

There are several bacteria and parasites that can cause illnesses that can harm an unborn baby.

Listeriosis Listeria is a genus of bacteria found in soil, water and some animals, including poultry and cattle, which can be present in raw milk and foods. Pregnant women are more susceptible to listeriosis than others, and it can lead to miscarriage and even stillbirth. You can contract listeriosis by eating undercooked meat or eggs, as well as certain cheeses.

Salmonella poisoning Salmonella is another group of bacteria that can cause food poisoning, which results in severe vomiting and diarrhoea. In order to prevent salmonella poisoning it's important to cook meat and eggs thoroughly and also have good hygiene techniques in the kitchen. Store fresh meat at the bottom of your fridge, and away from cooked meats. Don't prepare raw meat on the counter, use a chopping board and wipe it clean with hot soapy water straight after use.

Toxoplasmosis A warning to cat owners, toxoplasmosis is an infection caused by a tiny parasite that can live in cats, soil that has been contaminated by cat poo and in some foods. If a pregnant woman catches toxoplasmosis, her unborn baby can develop water on the brain (hydrocephalus) or brain damage. It can also damage the baby's eyes or other organs. You can prevent it by avoiding undercooked meats. If you have a cat, don't empty the cat litter tray and wear gardening gloves if you are digging in garden soil that could be contaminated. If you're worried that you may have been exposed to the infection, ask your midwife about a blood test.

Which supplements should I take during pregnancy?

It's really important to take multivitamin and mineral supplements during your pregnancy to ensure that your baby is getting all the nutrients it needs to grow. If you're trying to conceive it's a great time to start taking the multivitamin supplement and it's also worth continuing after the birth if you are breastfeeding.

While most vitamin and mineral supplements will vary slightly, it's important to choose one that contains at least 400 micrograms of folic acid and 10 micrograms of vitamin D as these are nutrients that we can't get as much from our diet. Vitamin A supplements should be avoided as too much of this vitamin can harm the baby. So choose a supplement that's meant for women during pregnancy as it won't contain vitamin A. Avoid any supplements with cod liver oil as these will contain vitamin A.

Do I need to take iron supplements?

Your body will increase its blood volume by 50 percent during pregnancy, so your body needs more iron to manufacture the substance in red blood cells called haemoglobin. While your body becomes more efficient at absorbing iron in pregnancy your doctor will probably recommend a prenatal supplement containing iron. Adding vitamin C to iron supplements will help your body absorb it – so a squeeze of lemon juice, orange juice, or a Vitamin C supplement will help you get the most out of your iron-rich foods or supplements.

Why do I need folic acid?

Folic acid is really important during pregnancy because it can help prevent neural tube defects such as spina bifida in your baby. It's essential to have enough in your first trimester, and because it's incredibly difficult to get it from your diet alone, a supplement is recommended (either on its own or in a multivitamin). Any woman who is trying for a baby should start taking folic acid, and continue throughout the pregnancy. The recommended amount of folic acid in your pregnancy is 400 micrograms per day.

What is the normal pregnancy weight gain?

Weight gain is something that pregnant women worry about a lot. Some women worry that their bump is too small and they are not putting on enough weight; others are concerned (generally for body image reasons) that they are putting on too much weight.

Over the course of your pregnancy you will need to put on weight, but this is not just 'fat'. You are growing a baby and in order to do this, your uterus will grow, the placenta will grow, your uterus will produce amniotic fluid, the volume of blood in your body increases, and of course there is the weight of your baby. All of this combined will cause you to put on weight.

However, for the first six months of pregnancy this does not mean you need to increase your normal calorie intake. In the last three months you only need to eat an extra 200 calories a day, which is just equivalent to small, healthy snack. It is very important to avoid empty calories such a sugary fizzy drinks and cakes and biscuits (see page 7) and to carry on with 30 minutes of light exercise a day, unless your doctor has advised you not to.

Are there any official guidelines for weight gain?

In the UK there are no official guidelines regarding weight gain. However, dieticians and doctors tend to adopt the US guidelines that say that a woman should be gaining around 12–16 kg (25–35 lb) over the course of her pregnancy if she is carrying one baby. You should gain more if you were underweight when you became pregnant or if you are carrying twins. There is no need to eat for two during pregnancy as gaining too much weight during pregnancy is not good for your overall health and may increase your risk for medical problems in pregnancy such as pre-eclampsia.

Around one in five women in the UK are obese when they become pregnant. Ideally if you are overweight (with a BMI over 30) it is recommended that you lose weight before getting pregnant, as being at a healthy weight would reduce your risk for various pregnancy complications such as miscarriage, pre-eclampsia, gestational diabetes and stillbirth. There is also evidence that if a mother is overweight before pregnancy her baby may be at increased risk of health problems in later life (these are called intergenerational health problems).

When should I be concerned?

If you do feel like you're not gaining enough weight, or you're gaining too rapidly, it's important to talk to your health visitor or doctor to find out why. If your bump is measuring small (roughly your bump should measure the equivalent centimetres for weeks of pregnancy, so at 30 weeks your bump should measure around 30 cm/12 in) you may be referred for an extra scan to assess your baby's growth and how much amniotic fluid can be measured around the baby.

Should I exercise during pregnancy?

Our bodies have evolved over hundreds of thousands of years to be able to remain active during pregnancy. Pregnancy is not a time to put your feet up and stop all activity (or eat for two). It is recommended that you take up to 30 minutes of gentle exercise a day throughout your pregnancy as long as you are well and haven't been advised to avoid any exercise.

If you haven't done much exercise previously we would recommend exercise that includes the whole body and is gentle without being too intensely aerobic or high impact. Yoga, Pilates and swimming are often preferred by women during pregnancy, and most areas have lots of classes. Aqua-natal yoga can be great too. When you are heavily pregnant it can be such a relief to go for a swim; it's great to feel weightless and cool in the water. Towards the end of pregnancy, it is generally recommended that you concentrate on gentle and holistic low-impact exercises like yoga, swimming and walking as it becomes harder to move and react than before.

If you played high-impact or dangerous sports before becoming pregnant, talk to your doctor and midwife and get advice from your sporting body about any risks to continuing your exercise routine.

What medical problems might prevent me exercising?

Some pregnant women are prescribed bed rest during pregnancy if they have a high-risk pregnancy that would be jeopardised by exercise: for example, women who have an 'incompetent cervix' or are at risk of preterm labour or a woman whose baby is not growing well due to inter-uterine growth restriction.

However, if you have any long-term medical problems such as asthma or hypertension, or physical problems that result from the pregnancy, talk to your doctor or antenatal team before taking up new exercise or carrying on with your usual exercise routine. Your body produces a hormone called relaxin, which softens your ligaments (the bands of tissue that hold joints together) in preparation for the birth. However, this can also cause some joints to be too loose, resulting in conditions such as symphosis pubis dysfunction/SPD (see page 68). If you have been diagnosed with SPD you will probably be advised to avoid exercise that causes the pelvis and/or the sacral joint to move or separate such as swimming breast-stroke, riding a bike and excessive walking or running.

Can I do exercises that prepare me for the birth?

Kegel or pelvic floor exercises are really important in pregnancy to increase strength and flexibility in the muscles surrounding the birth canal. If you are taking antenatal yoga or Pilates classes or active birth classes you will learn exercises that strengthen the pelvic floor. When you are out and about remember to contract and hold your pelvic floor muscles. You can do this while waiting at the bus stop or standing in a queue for the supermarket. The real trick is doing your pelvic floor exercises without pulling a face.

Is it common to find sleep difficult?

Many women find it harder to sleep during pregnancy and this gets worse as the bump gets bigger. Initially you may feel sick; later it becomes more difficult to get comfortable, you need to go to the bathroom for a wee and/or you may suffer from heartburn or leg cramps and 'restless' legs (see page 29).

What can I do to help?

First, try not to let it bother you if you can't sleep, and don't worry that it will harm your baby – it won't. If you can, nap during the day, and get some early nights during the week. Avoid drinking tea (even green tea), coffee or cola drinks in the evening as the caffeine can make it harder to go to sleep, whereas some foods can help sleep. Bananas and porridge, for example, contain tryptophan, the amino acid needed by the body to produce serotonin. Serotonin is used to make the sleep hormone melatonin.

Try to relax before bedtime so that you're not too wide awake. Avoid looking at tablets, smartphones and the television an hour before bedtime as the light stimulates the production of the stress hormone cortisol, which can stop you from sleeping. Relaxation techniques may also help. Your antenatal classes may teach relaxation techniques, or you could borrow a relaxation tape, CD or DVD from your library. Even if you're feeling tired during the day, try to get some activity, such as a walk at lunchtime or going swimming. Try joining an antenatal yoga class or Pilates class as exercise can help you to feel less tired and conversely help you to sleep. If the lack of sleep is bothering you, talk to your partner, a friend, doctor or midwife.

If your sleep problems are associated with discomfort try with sleeping with an extra pillow (to reduce heartburn) and a V-shaped pillow may help support your bump at night. These pillows come in useful for breastfeeding too so worth the investment.

Might there be a medical reason for insomnia?

Occasionally, sleeplessness – when accompanied by other symptoms – can be a sign of depression. If you have any of the other symptoms of depression, such as feeling hopeless and losing interest in the things you used to enjoy, speak to your doctor or midwife. There is treatment that can help. Find out more about mental health problems in pregnancy.

SLEEP HORMONES

There are two key hormones involved in sleep. Cortisol, the stress-response hormone, needs to be reduced to aid sleep, whereas production of melatonin, the sleep hormone needs to be increased. Cortisol release is triggered by daylight and is at its peak in the morning and should be reduced before bedtime to aid sleep; conversely, darkness and the cooler temperatures at the end of the day trigger melatonin.

When will I need to buy maternity clothes?

The short answer is – whenever you feel like it, or not. It varies quite a lot from woman to woman and how you are carrying your bump and what's happening with your breasts. Most women find they no longer fit into their 'normal' clothes sometime into the second trimester (around 14 to 16 weeks), or the end of first trimester for women having their second or third baby.

Remember Kate Moss wearing her regular jeans with the zipper open? Those jeans were her choice of maternity clothes, and very cool she looked too. Most of us won't be quite so brave. There is so much choice nowadays, from haute couture to supermarket brands or non-maternity clothes, so you can enjoy dressing for your new shape. Here are a few tips on what to wear:

- Jeans or loose trousers with an elasticated top are great – much more comfortable than firm trousers with buttons or zips. Tops that you can use to breastfeed with after the birth are a good idea.
- Normal clothes in bigger sizes can work too. However, if your pregnant shape is all bump, you may find that bigger sizes are too big across your shoulders so always try clothes on first.
- If your partner is bigger than you, wear his clothes for a while – a lovely cotton shirt can be really comfortable in the summer.
- Your feet might expand or grow – especially after the birth – so you might need to invest in some new shoes. In general, don't spend too

much (unless you really want to) since you'll only be wearing them for a short while.

- Don't feel that weddings and special events mean you have to hide under a tent-like dress, it can really give you confidence to have an outfit that celebrates your new shape.
- You can wear open trousers or skirts by using a 'belly button' or a 'bump band' (a simple device made from a piece of elastic with a button at either end – a hair scrunchy can also work) to widen the waistband. Wear a long T-shirt, a jumper pulled down over it, or a 'bellyband' (a wide stretchy band worn right around your waist) to hide the gap.
- Clothes made from stretchy fabric containing lycra are useful since they will 'stretch' with you as your bump grows. Clothes described as 'wrinkle free' or 'permanent press' are made from fabric treated with chemicals, and some women prefer to avoid them.

Will I need special bras?

It is worth investing in a maternity bra since it will be more comfortable. It's best not to wear an underwired bra as the wires may press against your developing milk ducts and restrict blood flow to the breasts. But unless you really prefer them, don't use your pre-pregnancy bras; buy a nice flexible one approved by a lactation consultant. If you are watching your spending you can buy a nursing bra while you are pregnant and wear that (although you may find that you need a bigger size in the weeks just after your baby is born and your milk comes in). It is worth getting your bra fitted by a specialist. However, you might want to invest in a pretty bra to celebrate your growing shape if you are enjoying the look and feel of your growing breasts.

What is antenatal depression?

Most of us have heard of postnatal depression, or PND, but we're not so familiar with antenatal depression, which happens to women during pregnancy. Antenatal depression is actually quite common, even in women who have planned their pregnancy and dearly want a baby. Around 20 percent of pregnant women will experience antenatal depression in some form or another. If you experience depression during your pregnancy then you are statistically more likely to experience PND after the birth.

There are huge changes in levels of hormones such as progesterone circulating in your body during pregnancy. Most pregnant women occasionally feel moody during pregnancy (with all the hormonal changes), or tired, or anxious. But if you're feeling sad, flat, lethargic and hopeless most of the time, you may have antenatal depression.

What should I do if I am feeling depressed?

If you think you are depressed during your pregnancy then it's important to take steps. The first things to do are the simplest ones:

- Talk to a friend or member of the family about how you feel.
- Eat healthily – if you're concerned about putting on weight get advice from a nutritionist – but essentially you should be eating a normal well-balanced diet with a couple of additional healthy snacks.
- Try to get enough sleep and rest.
- Join an antenatal group – sharing experiences and making new friends who are going through pregnancy with you now can really help.
- If you were on antidepressant medication before you became pregnant, talk to your doctor about whether you should continue to take it, don't just stop taking it.

How common is antenatal depression?

It is very common. You are more likely to experience antenatal depression if you have: a history of depression; family violence or substance abuse; no support; difficulties with your partner; or no partner. If you are feeling depressed and think it might be serious, or you can't manage it on your own, it's really important to get professional help; don't be embarrassed or worried to ask for help. Your doctor might suggest that you try a depression medication or cognitive behavioural therapy. Don't try self-medicating since some medicines are not suitable during pregnancy. In addition we recommend you contact the PANDAS Foundation for Pre- and Postnatal-Depression Advice and Support.

When is the best time to tell others that I am pregnant?

There are different reasons why and when you tell the different people in your life that you are expecting a baby. Many people wait until the end of the first trimester as the risk of miscarriage is highest during the first 12 weeks.

Telling close friends and family

It's really up to you to decide whether you want to tell them. Go with your instinct and do what you feel is best for you and your partner. Some women/couples prefer to wait until they have had the first scan that shows the baby's heartbeat, or at 12 weeks when they know everything seems fine. However, you might want to tell your family or friends earlier so you'll have their support if it does not go to plan and you miscarry. For the same reason, you might want to keep this private. You might be so excited that you want to tell your immediate family the day you have a positive test.

It can be difficult to know when to share your news with friends who are experiencing fertility problems or who are desperate to have a baby but are not in a relationship. However, don't tell them last as they may hear it second-hand, which would be even worse. Tell them in a straightforward way, preferably when you're on your own rather than in a group. Be sensitive to the number of excited updates you give them throughout your pregnancy and be led by their reactions. That's not to say that you should feel guilty for your joy and good fortune, just sensitive to how they might be feeling.

Telling work colleagues

With work colleagues, you may well decide not to tell them you're pregnant until the highest risk of miscarriage has passed and you have had your first scan so have a good idea of your due date. You might want to wait even longer, depending on your situation at work. Familiarise yourself with the maternity policies beforehand if you want to. When you do announce it, it's polite to tell your boss privately before announcing it to other colleagues. However, if you are suffering from extreme morning sickness, you might want to tell people earlier, so they'll understand why you're not up to par at work, or you're having to have days off. If your work involves any hazards that may affect your pregnancy, you must tell your boss as soon as you are pregnant. Do this, for example, if you work with hazardous substances or if you travel to tropical countries where you might need to take anti-malaria medication, as you will not be able to take it if you are pregnant.

Holding off until after your first scan might be your preference, since you can then avoid having to tell people if you suffer a miscarriage. However, if you do have a miscarriage you may want to tell your colleagues or work friends, as this is an upsetting and traumatic end to a pregnancy. You need to grieve for the death of the baby, and they can help; keeping it a secret is not always the best solution. However, each couple needs to make a decision based on their own situation.

When should I tell my other children?

Last but not least, when is the right time to tell your older children that they are going to have a little baby brother or sister? In general around the 12 weeks can work well but that is not to say that tiredness and morning sickness (or miscarriage), should be kept secret from your children. It does also depend on the child's age, but in general, the earlier you can tell your children, the sooner you can help them to prepare for the life change that a new baby will bring. It can help to focus on something that's going to make them happy when you tell them. For example – tell them that they are going to be a fantastic big sister or that they will be moving into a wonderful new big boy's bed. It can also help to buy them a doll or teddy that can be their 'new baby'. As the baby's due date nears, you can give your children exciting jobs such as choosing decorations or clothes for the new baby so that they feel involved.

When should I stop work?

In the past many women took their 'confinement' in the later stages of their pregnancy. The idea was that they rested and ate wholesome food to prepare for the birth of their baby. Today many women take the attitude that their pregnancy should have absolutely no impact on their normal working life. Furthermore, it's not uncommon for women to try to maximise their maternity leave to spend time with their baby, so they work right up until the last-possible moment.

In general, there is a happy medium but every woman's situation is different and all pregnant women will try to do what will work best for them. However, we would recommend taking as much time to rest and prepare before the birth as is possible for you. Take time to connect with your baby, think about the birth and gently nest.

If you are pregnant with twins or multiples you may be bigger than average and be more likely to go into labour a little early. For these reasons you may want to stop work earlier so that you get some time to rest and nest before your babies arrive.

The TAMBA (Twins and Multiple Births Association) report that mums recommend starting maternity leave between 28 and 30 weeks and earlier if you are carrying more than one baby or have any health complications.

How much time does my workplace need to plan my maternity leave?

If you tell work at around three months that will give them and you enough time to start discussing how your role will be filled while you're on maternity leave, and any other implications.

You also have the right to attend antenatal appointments so you shouldn't have to lie if you need to see your midwife or have a scan; just try and book appointments into your work diary at the easiest time for you and your colleagues. So if you always have a team meeting on Monday morning, don't book in all your midwife appointments then! The clinic will be aware that you have work commitments and should help you work around them and vice versa with your colleagues.

Is it safe to travel when I am pregnant?

Many women choose not to travel during the first trimester (12 weeks) because of morning sickness and tiredness, or the last trimester because of tiredness and the discomfort of sitting for any length of time. If you want to travel to a country where vaccinations or malaria tablets are required, talk to your doctor before booking. Some of the immunisations and malaria treatments are not suitable for pregnant women as they could harm the baby.

Can I travel by car?

Car travel is generally safe for both you and your expected baby but remember these points. Sitting in the car or driving a car may increase feelings of nausea and tiredness, especially in the early weeks. Road accidents occur sometimes with pregnant women for this reason. So try to avoid long trips as they can make you unusually tired. Share the driving, stop the car regularly and get out and walk about. Keep a bottle of water handy and open the windows a little if you can for fresh air. Put the seat belt under your bump over your lap – with the cross strap between your breasts. Do not put the belt over your bump.

What about flying?

Flying generally isn't considered harmful for you or your baby. But there are a few precautions to take.

- If you are travelling long-haul, there's a chance (even if you're not pregnant) of deep vein thrombosis (DVT). Drink lots of water, get up and walk around a lot, and wear special DVT socks you can buy at the airport or pharmacy while you are travelling.
- Once you are 28 weeks pregnant, an airline may request a letter from your doctor or midwife stating that you don't have a high-risk pregnancy and confirming your due date. Some airlines won't let you fly after 37 weeks (34 weeks if you are expecting twins) as there's a chance you'll go into labour on the flight.

Is it safe to have sex while I am pregnant?

The good news is that, generally speaking, it's perfectly safe to have sex while you're pregnant. You may even find that your libido really increases at certain times during your pregnancy and your partner may love your pregnant shape.

However, follow your own instincts and do what feels right for you both. If you have experienced some bleeding during early pregnancy and/or have had a previous miscarriage, then you may feel more comfortable abstaining from sex for a while during this time. That said, it's now recognised that if a miscarriage is going to occur, it will do so whether you have sex beforehand or not. If you've taken a long time to conceive, you really might feel like you want to be very careful during early pregnancy. Similarly some men might feel nervous about causing a miscarriage or harming the baby in some way. The evidence says it is safe but you will need to understand your partner's anxiety and be patient. If your partner does feel very nervous about having sex, he probably won't enjoy it and may experience anxiety or stress worrying about it afterwards.

Are some positions better?

Opt for positions that are comfortable to you, your bump and your cervix. Having your partner spooning from behind when your bump is big allows you to lie on your side and the penetration isn't so deep.

However, you both may enjoy more cuddling during this time too, especially towards the end of your pregnancy when you may feel very uncomfortable and tired. If you use massage oils, make sure that you do not use essential oils that are not safe for pregnancy, such as black pepper, rosemary and clary sage.

Can sex help if the baby is overdue?

Sex and nipple stimulation are sometimes recommended when a woman is overdue. The theory is that nipple stimulation stimulates hormones that can help labour to begin naturally.

What substances can harm my unborn baby?

Some prescription medicines can affect your unborn baby, so speak to your doctor before you start planning to conceive or as soon as you are pregnant as it may be possible to change them. Recreational drugs, cigarettes, and alcohol can also seriously harm your baby.

How do cigarettes and smoking affect a baby?

Smoking during pregnancy is the single biggest risk factor in causing Sudden Infant Death Syndrome (SIDS) in newborn babies. Cigarettes contain over 400 chemicals and every time you smoke a cigarette it harms your baby. If you smoke, your risk of miscarriage is greater and it can lead to the formation of blood clots. Smoking also raises your baby's heart rate and the likelihood of fetal abnormalities.

If you are a smoker and want to stop smoking because of pregnancy, talk to your midwife. He or she can be able to refer you to a smoking cessation counsellor. There is also an NHS Smoking Healthline.

Is alcohol safe in moderation?

No, it isn't. Drinking alcohol may affect an unborn baby as some alcohol will pass through the placenta. Alcohol may increase the chance of miscarriage and cause other fetal damage. The Royal College of Obstetricians and Gynaecologists (RCOG) used to say that it was acceptable to drink a couple of glasses of wine (or equivalent number of units) per week.

However, the RCOG has revised this advice and in February 2015 made an announcement that there is no proven amount of alcohol that is safe for the developing fetus. This advice is in line with previous National Institute for Health and Care Excellence (NICE) recommendations, which recommends no alcohol, particularly in the first trimester of pregnancy. Abstinence is the only way to be certain that your developing baby or fetus is not harmed.

I drank alcohol before I realised I was pregnant – what should I do?

Pregnant women often worry that they have drunk alcohol before they knew they were pregnant. Luckily pregnancy tests today give women a positive test very early in the pregnancy. If you are concerned, talk to your doctor or midwife and don't be embarrassed – this is a question they get asked on a daily basis by newly pregnant women.

What is fetal alcohol spectrum disorder?

This is an umbrella term used to describe a range of effects – physical, mental, behavioural – that can occur in a baby whose mother drank alcohol during pregnancy. These disorders can have lifelong impact on a child's development and may even affect a child's facial features in incidences of high levels of alcohol intake.

How does caffeine affect an unborn baby?

Caffeine consumption should be limited during pregnancy and UK guidelines suggest that the maximum amount is 200 mg per day. This is the equivalent of one really strong cup of coffee, two cups of instant coffee or three cups of tea (green tea also contains caffeine). Some fizzy drinks and chocolate will also contain caffeine and should be limited. If you like to drink tea or coffee and want more than this during your pregnancy, choose a decaffeinated version. Interestingly quite a number of tea- and coffee-loving women report they completely go off their favourite drink and often opt for naturally caffeine-free teas like mint tea and chamomile tea. One theory is that morning sickness and pregnancy taste changes are natural defence systems that prevent you from consuming harmful substances in order to protect your developing fetus. This is especially important in the first trimester, when the baby would be most susceptible to toxins and substances in food.

I am on prescription drugs for a medical condition. Will they be safe?

If you need to take prescription drugs, your doctor or pharmacist should be able to recommend or prescribe an option that is safe to use during pregnancy. It can be difficult because most pharmaceutical companies don't carry out extra tests to assess whether their drugs are safe to use during pregnancy or while breastfeeding. So they often add a generic label saying that the medication is 'not suitable for use in pregnancy or while nursing'. In some cases you will be advised to stop taking your usual prescription drugs altogether during pregnancy. Don't take any over-the-counter drugs during pregnancy without first asking your doctor or pharmacist for advice.

What are the most common symptoms of pregnancy?

Pregnancy involves huge physical changes in your anatomy, physiology and endocrine system (hormone production). Along with these changes come some very common pregnancy ailments that affect some women more than others. There will be times when you absolutely love your new body shape with your lovely round and firm bump, your clear skin and perhaps your bigger breasts. Then at other times you will feel like you don't recognise your body at all and you feel exhausted, especially if you are suffering with some of the less glamorous pregnancy symptoms such as piles (see below). It can also be really tough if you have a high-risk pregnancy or develop painful problems like symphosis pubis dysfunction (see page 68), or extreme morning sickness (hyperemesis gravidarum, see page 69).

Don't be put off. Lots of women actually feel better and more energetic during pregnancy and hardly anyone suffers with all the symptoms at the same time. Be kind to your amazing body – it's growing a new baby.

Why am I out of breath?

In the early days and weeks especially, the growing fetus, placenta and uterus need a lot of oxygen. So you may find yourself breathing faster, and often feeling out of breath. You will actually make more blood and in the early stages of pregnancy you might notice that your circulatory system improves.

PREGNANCY HORMONES

The hormones that are important during pregnancy include: human chorionic gonadotropin (or hCG), progesterone, oestrogen, relaxin, oxytocin, prolactin, and a group of hormones called endorphins.

You may experience constipation, nausea and heartburn because of the changes in your digestive system triggered by the hormone levels. Mood changes are also common, you might feel a bit depressed or tearful, or more grumpy than usual. Sometimes these changes can be quite extreme. Many of the hormone levels drop suddenly after the birth – and this may contribute to feelings of depression.

In early pregnancy
- hCG helps prepare the womb, and can produce morning sickness and tiredness.
- Progesterone and oestrogen help release the egg from your ovaries and implant it in your womb, increasing blood supply.
- Progesterone helps the baby grow and can cause upset tummies, bloating, sore breasts and legs – even unwanted hair growth.
- Relaxin is a hormone produced by both the placenta and the ovaries. During pregnancy it relaxes the ligaments in the pelvis and widens and softens the cervix to make the birth easier. Other muscles in your body may also relax, which might make you ache a little, and might effect your pelvic floor muscles so you may need to go to the loo all the time.

In later pregnancy
- Oxytocin creates the bonding feeling and can lead to strong urges to rush around to create a 'nest' for your new baby.
- Oxytocin triggers labour, as well as stretching the cervix and stimulating the breasts to produce milk.
- Prolactin is the milk-producing hormone and also has a tranquilising effect. It prepares the breasts for breastfeeding.

As your baby grows, your bump will get bigger, pushing your stomach, intestines and other organs out of place. Usually they get pushed upwards – another reason you'll feel out of breath – since your ribcage and diaphragm are restricted so you cannot breathe in and out as deeply as you could before. However, this change is gradual so you will get used to it; walking up a flight of stairs may take you by surprise as you may feel incredibly breathless and light-headed.

Does my heart rate increase too?

Your blood volume increases to carry the additional oxygen around your body. More blood vessels are formed to carry this increased blood flow. Your heart rate might increase and so you may experience a racing heart when you do something even mildly physically taxing. You are now officially breathing for two.

Why do I feel so tired?

Your body is diverting a huge amount of energy to the development of your baby – so it should be no surprise if you feel tired. The frustrating thing for many women is that they feel most exhausted in those early weeks where they have no bump and perhaps haven't yet told friends and colleagues. If you have a big commute on public transport it can be really tough, so don't be shy to ask for a seat. Wear a badge saying 'Baby on Board' and people will usually give you a seat. The sooner you can tell your colleagues and friends, the sooner they can help you. Remember, as well as everything else you are doing, you are growing a new human being so give yourself a literal and metaphorical break.

Often women report that they feel full of energy in their second trimester. However, as they enter the third trimester, fatigue can come back with a vengeance – although at this stage people can see your bigger bump and they will hopefully offer to help you. If you are carrying twins or if you have a very physical job it may make sense for you to start your maternity leave a little sooner than other pregnant women. If this is not possible, ask your employers to allow you to focus on less strenuous or stressful work in these last weeks.

How common is morning sickness?

So-called morning sickness is really common during pregnancy. It's characterised by nausea and vomiting and, while it can be worst in the first trimester (12 weeks), some women suffer from it throughout their pregnancy. Don't be fooled by thinking that morning sickness is only confined to the morning, as many women will feel symptoms all day. It is caused by changes in your hormones, which may also give you a heightened sense of smell and taste. One theory is that these heightened senses allow you to avoid toxins that may damage your developing baby, especially in the vulnerable first 12 weeks.

In order to help manage symptoms of morning sickness, try eating small, frequent meals. Always having a little food in your stomach can help alleviate the symptoms, as can an adequate fluid intake and plenty of sleep. Although not scientifically based, some women find fresh ginger or even a ginger biscuit helps.

A few women experience a very severe version of morning sickness called hyperemesis gravidarum (see page 69) and may require hospital treatment.

Why do I have swollen feet and hands?

Many women suffer from swollen ankles and feet in pregnancy as the body copes with the extra fluids in your circulation. Try to avoid standing up for too long and use a body brush in the shower or bath to help with lymphatic drainage – gently brush your skin back towards your heart especially on your arms and legs. Swollen feet, hands and ankles are generally harmless, but if the swelling comes on suddenly as is accompanied by a bad headache, problems with your vision, vomiting or pain under your ribs you need call your doctor or antenatal clinic urgently to rule out pre-eclampsia (see page 66).

Why do I feel bloated and keep suffering from heartburn?

Things can feel very uncomfortable and unpleasant with your tummy. Even if you've always been regular and had a happy digestive system, you may now suffer with constipation, wind and bloating. Heartburn is also very common as the hormone relaxin that softens and loosens the ligaments in your pelvis for birth can 'weaken' the sphincter at the top of your stomach. This means the contents of your stomach (containing acid) can 'leak' back up your oesophagus (food pipe), especially when you are lying down. Speak to your doctor about safe heartburn treatments. You can try sleeping slightly propped up with an extra pillow, avoid very spicy foods (especially before exercise or going to sleep) and don't lie down straight after you have eaten.

Bloating can occur because of the increased levels of progesterone, which slows down your digestion, giving nutrients more time to enter your bloodstream and be delivered to your baby. This can also lead to constipation. Try to include foods such as figs, apricots and beetroot and drink a lot of water. If constipation becomes a problem speak to your doctor but make sure he or she knows that you are pregnant.

Is vaginal discharge normal?

When you're not pregnant, it is normal for your vagina to produce a clear or white discharge. This happens because your cervix constantly sheds cells, which are replaced by new ones. During pregnancy this discharge can increase as a way of flushing out potential infections that could travel up the vagina, through the cervix and into the uterus.

If your discharge has a colour or an unusual smell or if your vaginal area feels sore or itchy you need to get yourself checked out as you may have an infection. If you have thrush, discuss the best treatment with your doctor. Avoid tight knickers made of artificial materials (loose cotton underwear is best) and don't use soaps and shower gels as they may make the problem worse. Tell your midwife or doctor if the discharge increases a lot in later pregnancy. It can sometimes be confused with urine so it can help to keep samples to show your midwife.

In the last days of your pregnancy, as your body gets ready for labour, you may get your 'show' – a thicker discharge that may contain a bit of blood and darker mucus. This is a plug of material that comes away as the uterus prepares to start contracting and opening the cervix to allow your baby to pass into the birth canal. You may get several shows before you go into labour.

What if I notice spotting or bleeding?

It can be quite common for women to find a spotting of blood in their underwear when they are pregnant. This is usually nothing to worry about. However, blood loss sometimes indicates a problem with the placenta or can be an early sign of miscarriage so you need to call your antenatal team straight away. Let the midwife know if you have any accompanying cramping pains too. Take a sample of your underwear with you if you have changed before you visit them.

My mood changes very rapidly. Is this normal?

Mood swings in pregnancy are very common. They are partly caused by changes in hormones. If you have suffered with pre-menstrual syndrome you may be familiar with the powerful feelings of sadness and anger. These mood swings are most common in the first 12 weeks of pregnancy and the feelings and your responses can feel alien to you and out of your control. Try to be kind to yourself and remember that pregnancy and preparing for the arrival of a new baby is a huge upheaval in life. Although millions of people become new parents every year it is still probably the biggest life event we go through. It's really important to get lots of rest. Keep things simple and accept support from your loved ones. If you are concerned about your feelings, it's really important to talk to your partner, friends, midwife or doctor.

Why are my breasts so tender and swollen?

The changes in your breasts will probably be one of the things that you (and people around you) notice early on. Before pregnancy a woman's breasts are in a kind of suspended animation; they only become 'fully functional' during pregnancy.

As soon as you become pregnant, the blood supply to your breasts increases so that the milk-making tissue grows. You will probably notice a big increase in size. They will probably feel tender because of the rising levels of oestrogen and progesterone. You may also notice blue veins near the surface as the blood flow to your breasts increases. The blood also supplies them with the nutrients, immune factors, growth factors and water needed for milk production. Your nipples may stick out more and darken, in preparation for breastfeeding. Towards the end of your pregnancy, you may even leak a little of the first breastmilk, called colostrum, especially if this is not your first baby. If your breasts feel very uncomfortable and swollen, try putting a Savoy cabbage leaf in your bra; lots of women find that it is refreshing and cools things down a bit. This can also help later when you are breastfeeding.

I keep getting hot flushes; is this normal?
Yes, it is. The hormone changes through pregnancy can cause all sorts of changes including 'hot flushes'. You may also feel warmer because you have increased blood volume and a better peripheral circulation. Whereas before you had to wear socks in bed and gloves outside, now you may feel very warm and find centrally heated rooms unbearable. Make sure you wear layers to you can layer up or down as your body temperature fluctuates.

Why do I need to wee all the time?
The pregnancy hormone human chorionic gonadotropin (hCG), produced by the cells of the placenta as they embed into the uterine wall, increases the blood flow to your kidneys. This allows your kidneys to get rid of the increased amount of waste products being produced by you and your baby. Later on in pregnancy your expanding uterus puts a lot of pressure on the bladder, urethra and pelvic floor muscles. This may lead to temporary bladder-control problems, particularly once the baby's head is engaged (see page 37), and you just feel the need to go for a wee endlessly night and day. So you are now weeing for two.

My back aches; is that normal?
As your baby grows your spine will realign slightly to maintain balance with the increased weight in the front. This can cause temporary back pain and make you throw your weight backwards and waddle slightly. Try to go swimming, as not only will you be weightless, but it will also take the pressure off your back. Exercises like antenatal yoga and Pilates can help you strengthen your body as it changes during pregnancy.

Will I get stretch marks?

These are caused when the dermis (underneath the upper epidermis layer of the skin) is stretched by rapid growth. They are very common and can appear during puberty when we have a growth spurt. Women's bodies grow very quickly during pregnancy and this can cause little tears in the dermis. Stretch marks start out as either a red, pinkish, purplish colour and seem to be a bit of a genetic lottery. Some women will get lots across their tummy, breasts and hips and others don't get any. They tend to appear after the second trimester. Over time they fade to a pale white, and if you have pale skin you will hardly notice them.

Are there other likely skin changes?

Hormone changes can cause changes in skin colour in some women, or hyperpigmentation. It is more common in darker-skinned women and runs in families. The linea nigra is perhaps the most noticeable area of pigmentation and is caused by the increased production of melatonin. It can appear as a dark line that runs from the tummy button down to the top of your pubic hair. Darker patches of skin can occur on your nipples, face, genitals and under your arms. This pigmentation usually fades a few months after your baby is born. Protect your skin from the sun by wearing a wide-brimmed hat, use a sunscreen or sunblock (chose one that does not contain retinol) and avoid sunbeds. Some women can develop spider veins on their skin and reddening of the palms. The increased blood and circulation to your skin can give you a real glow of health and the legendary pregnancy 'bloom'.

Will pregnancy affect my hair and nails?

Hormone changes may cause temporary changes in the texture of your hair and nails. Women will often be complemented on their hair during pregnancy and nails may become harder, more brittle or softer. They will begin to return to normal a few months after your baby is born. You may find that normal hair shedding decreases towards the end of pregnancy so your hair will appear thicker. After birth, you may begin to lose all that hair that didn't fall out during your pregnancy.

Chapter 2: Your growing baby

Most prospective mums and dads love to know exactly what's going on inside mum's growing tummy and every parent and baby's bonding journey is unique. It's an everyday miracle and it's fascinating to track your baby's development from conception to birth. Following your baby's changes also helps you to prepare to be a parent too.

In this chapter we outline what's happening to your baby in each of the three stages, or trimesters, of pregnancy. Important basics such as determining your due date, as well as what happens if your baby is premature are all covered. All the work done by The Essential Parent Company focuses very strongly on parent-baby bonds. Even before your baby is born, you can start thinking about bonding and understanding how your hormones will help you become a loving parent to your developing baby. This will be a huge help in preparing for the birth.

What are the three trimesters of pregnancy?

Your pregnancy 'officially' starts from the first day of your last menstrual period. Obviously it might 'really' start quite a bit later than that, and you may even know exactly when your baby was conceived. Your 'dating' scan (see page 50) can also help determine the real date as well as your baby's potential due date.

Your pregnancy should last around 40 weeks, or nine months, and is divided, medically speaking, into three stages, known as trimesters. The first trimester is the first third of the pregnancy, or weeks one to 12. The second trimester is the middle section, weeks 13 to 27. The third trimester is the last stage, weeks 28 to 40 (the birth).

How mums feel in each trimester varies enormously (see page 69). Some women will sail through all three stages with no nausea and little tiredness. Others will feel morning sickness from the very beginning, and suddenly start to feel better at the end of the first trimester, but a few suffer from it right through to the birth. Most women find they need to wee a lot more often, and many go off certain foods. You may get out of breath more easily, especially as the pregnancy progresses, since your baby will start to push up into your lung space.

We've given a general overview of each trimester here, but you are the expert on yourself and your pregnancy so try to listen gently to your body at each stage.

What's happens during the first trimester?

How you feel The first trimester can be exhausting as your body changes physiologically to grow and develop your baby – your metabolic rate speeds up and your heart and breathing rate increase to cope. It's no wonder you feel so tired. It is also in these first 12 weeks that women report that their morning sickness and food-preference changes peak (you may have cravings and aversions to some foods). You will be offered your first dating scan at eight to 14 weeks and will see your baby for the first time.

Your baby The baby is growing at a tremendous rate in this trimester. Your baby begins as a few cells – you probably won't even be aware that you are pregnant. The fertilised egg becomes a bundle of cells, which travels along the fallopian tube and at around day six attaches to the wall of your uterus in a process called 'implantation'. The amniotic sac, umbilical cord and placenta grow. All the major organs start to develop, as well as the beginnings of the spinal cord, and the heart will start to beat around day 25. Little buds start to form, which will develop into limbs, and by 12 weeks, hands and fingers, feet and toes and ears will be visible. By the end of the first trimester, all being well, your baby will be around 6 cm (2 in) long and will weigh about 28 g (1 oz).

What's happens during the second trimester?

How you feel This is the stage when women feel they are blooming, their energy levels return to normal, they have a small but definite bump and often don't feel as sick or tired as before. Some women start to get heartburn at this stage as the ligaments relax (see pages 29-30). Many women start to feel their baby moving from about 20 weeks, though you may not feel regular movement until about 24 weeks. Some women feel fluttering earlier than that – at say 16 weeks. Between 18 and 21 weeks you will have another scan.

    Your baby During the second trimester, the baby will start to move around and kick more. By month five, he should be very active – he can usually move from side to side and may even turn upside down. The baby also starts to have periods of being asleep, which you'll probably learn to recognise as well. By the end of the second trimester, your baby will be between 20 and 30 cm (8 and 12 in) in length and weigh about 454 g (1 lb). Babies can survive from 24 weeks in neonatal intensive care units (see page 38).

What's happens during the third trimester?

How you feel The third trimester can become increasingly tiring as you are carrying around an ever-bigger baby. You might start to feel quite uncomfortable with heartburn, haemorrhoids, swollen ankles, warm body temperature and tiredness. Your breasts may put on another final growth spurt and as the breast tissue develops, your breasts may leak colostrum (this happens earlier in some pregnant women while others will not produce any colostrum until after their baby is born). As your belly grows you may notice the appearance of stretch marks. Despite all of this, the third trimester is a period of great excitement and planning, as the birth of your baby is imminent. This is when your nesting might really kick in and you will feel a burst of energy as you plan and prepare for your baby's arrival.

    Your baby During the third trimester, the baby begins to open and close his eyes, and respond to sound and light. His brain is now fully developed, but his lungs are still developing. As the weeks progress there is less and less room in the womb for him to move. By about weeks 35 to 36 your baby will move into his birth position, usually head down, and stay there, tightly packed in. His head may move down into the pelvis, or engage, ready for birth (see pages 39, 101).

Should I monitor my baby's movement?
It's important to monitor your baby's movements once you start to become aware of them. You will soon find there is a rhythm to them. Call your midwife if your baby's movements change. An easy thing to do if you are worried is lie down quietly after eating and count ten movements by your baby. Reduced movement can be your early warning that your baby needs to be born a bit earlier than planned.

How does a baby develop?

From the minute that the sperm penetrates the egg, you and your partner's genes combine to create a unique human being. Over the next 40 weeks, or nine months, in your uterus, this new baby will grow and mature, ready for her arrival in the world. Here is an approximate overview of this amazing process.

First week Sperm fertilises the egg and forms one cell smaller than a grain of sand (zygote). Over the next few days the cell divides rapidly as it travels down your fallopian tubes and into your uterus. The fertilised egg, now called a blastocyst and consisting of 150-300 cells, implants in the womb lining.

Two weeks The blastocyst essentially divides into two parts: cells of the outer part form the placenta, while the inner part develops into the fetus.

Three weeks The placenta and umbilical cord are now doing their job of delivering nutrition to the embryo, and the neural tube begins to develop – this will become the brain, spinal cord and nervous system.

Four weeks The tiny embryo is now about the size of a poppy seed.

Five weeks Your baby's heart is already dividing into chambers, and the major organs will start to develop. Little buds that will become the limbs start to appear.

Six weeks Your baby's brain now begins to control movement of the muscles and organs. She looks like a tadpole with a body and a tail.

Seven weeks The brain hemispheres are growing. There are dark spots where the nostrils and eyes are forming. The lenses are forming in the eyes. The jaw starts to show teeth buds up in the gums. Ears are starting to develop.

Nine weeks Your baby is about the size of an olive and starting to look human; she's lost her 'tail' and has a more obvious head. Hands and feet continue to form along with the fingers, toes and elbows - internal organs such as testes and ovaries start to develop. Eyelids will be completely fused over your baby's eyes.

12 weeks The 'embryo' is now officially a 'fetus' and is about the size of a plum. Your baby is swallowing amniotic fluid and passing urine. Wrists and ankles and tiny finger and toenails are present.

14 weeks In baby boys the prostate gland is developing and the ovaries of baby girls are descending from the abdomen to the pelvis. Your baby's thyroid gland starts producing important hormones for growth and metabolism and her hair starts to grow. She will now be about 8 cm (3 in) length.

16 weeks Your baby is now around 10 cm (4 in) long – the size of an avocado pear. She can swallow, hiccup, kick and swim. Your bump will probably start to show at around this point.

20 weeks Up until now, your baby has been measured from 'crown to rump' – but now she will be measured from crown to heel. At 20 weeks she'll be around 26 cm (10 in) long and growing fast. Your baby will be growing the waxy covering called vernix, which coats and protects her skin and makes the birth easier.

24 weeks Your baby weighs around 600 g (21 oz) and is approximately 30 cm (12 in) long. All her main organs are now working, except for her lungs, which remain dormant until she takes her first breath. Your baby responds to sounds outside the uterus and her fingerprints are forming. If she was born now she could survive with proper care.

30 weeks At this age most babies move into a head-down position, but may not stay there before 34 weeks and are almost at their final birth length; however their brain continues to develop at a rapid pace.

Mum may feel powerful kicks under her ribcage. By now your baby can open and shut her eyes. At this point she will be around 40 cm (15 in) long and weigh around 1.3 kg (2 lb 8 oz)

34 weeks Your baby's toenails will have reached the tip of her toes and the umbilical cord will be about 45 cm (18 in) long. Your baby will be getting fatter now too and will weigh around 2 kg (4 lb 8 oz).

36 weeks All the senses are now well-developed, although your baby's eyesight will improve rapidly in the weeks after birth. She will be sensitive to hot and cold and pressure. She will be gaining a huge amount of weight – around 28 g (1 oz) a day. Your baby now weighs nearly 3 kg (6 lb 6 oz) and will be nearly 50 cm (19 in) from head to toe.

40 weeks Your baby is fully developed and ready to be born. Her hair might already be thick. Over 95 percent of babies are head-down in the uterus and will be born this way. The average weight of a newborn at term is about 3.4 kg (7 lb 5 oz), although anything between 2.5 kg (5 lb 5 oz) and 4 kg (8 lb 8 oz) is considered normal.

How does my body feed and nurture my baby?

Like other mammals, a woman's body has evolved over millions of years to nurture the baby inside her body safely and provide him with all the oxygen and nutrients he needs over the 40 weeks in the uterus.

When you conceive, the fertilised egg travels down one of your fallopian tubes and into the uterus. There the embryo, now called a blastocyst, lands on the surface of the uterus, which has a rich blood supply. The blastocyst burrows into the lining of your uterus and some of its cells begin to form the life-support system – the placenta – that supplies the oxygen and energy needed to make the miraculous change from a few hundred cells to a fully developed baby. The remaining outer cells will develop into the baby.

The placenta grafts itself onto the lining of the uterus. It allows oxygen and energy (fats, carbohydrates, proteins) to pass from your blood into your baby's developing circulatory system via the umbilical cord, which is attached to your baby at his belly button. Your baby's lungs will not work until he is born and takes his first breath; until then you supply all his oxygen. All of your baby's waste products are passed into the umbilical cord, through the placenta, and back into your bloodstream, for your body to dispose of. This means your baby doesn't actually 'poo' until after he is born.

What happens if my baby is premature?

If a baby is born very early he will need medical help to feed and sometimes to breathe. An incubator in the special care baby unit (SCBU) does its best to replicate the mother's body by providing warmth, oxygen and food until the baby is able to breastfeed, breathe and regulate his own body temperature (see pages 134, 138).

If your baby is born prematurely your body can help regulate his body temperature and breathing by skin-to-skin contact. Known as 'kangaroo care' this was originally trialled in Equador when there was an incubator shortage. The method was found to be the best way to regulate a baby's body temperature and breathing. So you can still help to support your baby even after a premature birth. Your body will also start producing milk (lactating) earlier, so that when your baby is able to suck you can breastfeed him. Before that the precious colostrum you produce will be perfect food for your premature baby. You can express it and feed it to him via a tiny syringe.

Will my baby be born on the due date?

Doctors and midwives calculate due dates by taking the first day of your last period as day one and the due date as 40 weeks from that point. This is called 'at term', when a baby is considered to be fully developed. This is most accurate for women with a regular 28-day menstrual cycle as it assumes that ovulation and fertilisation occur approximately 14 days after that date. First-time mums might be more likely to go overdue. Older mothers over the age of 40 are also more likely to have longer pregnancies and there has been a 15 percent increase in mothers of this age group.

Statistically speaking, there's only about a four to five percent chance that your baby will be born exactly on her due date. Around 80 percent of women deliver anywhere between 38 and 42 weeks after first day of their last period. Around 11 percent of women give birth to their baby prematurely – before 37 weeks of pregnancy. Some of these women go into labour spontaneously and sometimes there is a medical reason why these babies are delivered early, either by Caesarian section or by artificial induction of the birth (see page 108). In addition, multiple pregnancies tend to deliver earlier than 40 weeks. Women who are underweight women are more likely to deliver early too.

Births after 42 weeks are called 'post-term.' Around four percent of pregnancies last longer than 42 weeks. At that point, hospitals usually induce labour as the rates of stillbirth increase after this time and the pros of induction are largely thought to exceed the pros of letting the pregnancy take its natural course. However, induced births carry their own risks and are often difficult for women to cope with, as the contractions can be very strong.

Will the dating scan give a different date?

As we have said, your due date is calculated as 40 weeks (or 280 days) after the first day of your last menstrual period (LMP), but the time of conception has a fairly wide window after that date. Even if you think you know the exact date of conception, the length of pregnancy can vary a great deal. After your dating scan (see pages 58) your due date may be updated, since it often gives a more accurate reading.

How will I be a good mum to my baby?

At some point in the pregnancy almost every expectant mum panics that she won't be up to the job of motherhood. Even as your bump grows it can be hard to imagine what your baby will look like or what being a mum and caring for a baby will entail. Don't worry; even if you've never been a broody person or spent any time thinking and hoping you would have a family, rest assured that millions of years of evolution have led to ways of helping women become mothers. We outline some of these natural changes below.

How important are hormones?

A lot of the processes that help you make the change from adult woman to mum are neurological and begin in pregnancy. The pituitary gland in the brain (often called the 'master gland', because it controls hormone release around the body) stimulates the production of pregnancy hormones. These play an important role in the process of bonding after the birth.

What changes take place in the brain?

For new mothers, some of the starkest differences are also the most intimate ones – the emotional changes. These changes result from growth and activity in regions of the brain that control bonding, empathy, anxiety, and social interaction.

Psychologists and neuroscientists have been very interested to understand what happens in our brains to help us love our new baby and be good, careful parents. Part of this research has been looking at why these feelings can spill over and become problems – for example, obsessively checking to see if a baby is breathing, severe anxiety and postnatal depression. Most new parents in the animal kingdom stop behaving as they did before they had babies and become generally obsessed with their babies: they check them, clean them and feed them constantly.

Neuroscientists have observed that changes in the parts of the brain that regulate basic emotions like fear, anxiety and aggression – the amygdala – drive both empathy and obsessive-compulsive behaviours. The amygdala is an almond-shaped mass of cells located deep within the brain's temporal lobe. In new mums the amygdala becomes more sensitive and fires more often to drive caring and checking behaviour. It fires much more when we look at or hold our own baby (compared to a stranger's baby). This heady cocktail of neurological activity helps new mums and dads to love, understand and care for their babies.

How do we produce the right hormones?

Luckily, our mummy brains reward us more too, so that looking into the eyes of our new baby activates the reward centres of the brain, giving us a pleasurable release of dopamine. In addition, feeding, cuddling and talking to our new baby releases the hormone oxytocin, which promotes bonding and makes us feel more relaxed, calm and happy around our new baby. It's like a positive-feedback loop: the more you cuddle and care for your baby, the more oxytocin you produce, which strengthens your bond and makes you want to care and cuddle your baby even more. It happens to dads too.

The good news for pregnant women is that oxytocin production dramatically increases during pregnancy, so that by the time your baby is born you are neurologically primed to become a mother. Some mothers experience a huge oxytocin boost at the birth and report a thunderclap moment of bonding and blissful love. If it doesn't happen to you, don't worry; bonding is a process, not a one-off event, and the deep and unique bond we have with our children develops and deepens over the weeks and months of pregnancy and early parenthood. Breastfeeding also stimulates oxytocin production. If you're bottle-feeding, make sure to use lots of skin-to-skin contact and a lot of cuddling as well so you don't miss out on the bonding experience.

How can I encourage bonding with my baby during pregnancy?

The bond with your baby can begin for you as soon as you find out you are going to have a baby. In the early days you will anticipate cuddling, feeding and caring for your baby.

When you first feel your baby move (this may not happen until about 16 to 20 weeks in first-time mums) you will experience a deep and intimate connection with your little baby that no one else is aware of. It can be lovely to take some time to either lie on your bed or in a warm bath and concentrate on feeling your baby moving. Babies tend to move more when you are lying still as the rocking movement of you walking around is thought to make them sleep, just as it does after they are born.

By 23 weeks your baby can also hear your voice and perceive pressure so take time to relax, stroke your belly and talk and sing to your baby. When your baby moves or kicks, stroke her, talk to her or gently push back. You can begin a lovely two-way communication when she responds to your pushes. Some mums have even reported that the lullabies that they sang to their babies in the womb are the ones they find most soothing as babies. It can be really nice to remember the songs and lullabies from your childhood and pass them on to your baby now.

Try massaging your bump while you focus on your growing baby. If you use massage oil, chose one with a basic carrier oil that is suitable for pregnant women. Essential oils such as clary sage and rosemary are not suitable for pregnancy.

Should I go to an antenatal class?

Going to an antenatal class with other pregnant women or couples can also really help you to bond. When you spend time with other expectant mums it gives you the mental space to talk about and enjoy this wonderful time as your baby grows and develops inside you. There are lots of classes to join, such as aquanatal yoga, antenatal yoga (which usually includes meditation and relaxation), antenatal Pilates and even antenatal birth classes that allow you and your partner to talk about and anticipate the arrival of your new baby. Enjoy this time and see it as an important beginning in the life-long bond that you will share with your baby.

How can my partner get involved with my pregnancy and our baby?

Many women feel that their partners are not as involved in the baby during pregnancy as they are. This is partly down to biology and physiology. Until your bump starts to show, it can be very hard for your partner to believe that his baby will be born in a matter of months. However, that is not to say that your partner cannot be excited, moved and full of anticipation at the arrival of the baby. Fathers can focus their energy on supporting their pregnant partner, as it is her body that is providing nourishment and oxygen to grow their baby. The energy required for a man to fertilise the egg has been calculated as being about the same as energy required to boil an egg. The biological mother provides the energy to create every cell in the baby's body. This requires a lot of energy and has been estimated that it is equivalent to the energy required to run 20 marathons. Helping to nurture you can help your partner feel more involved, and it is lovely for you to feel supported and cherished by your partner.

Going to antenatal classes together can help your partner feel involved during pregnancy and he can meet other people in the same situation (see page 44). Birth partners hate to feel helpless during labour and these classes are also about preparing your birth partner to be able to help you relax and be comfortable in the run-up to the birth, during labour and after your new baby arrives. If you feel that all the responsibility is on your shoulders, you can encourage your partner to share the tasks, maybe by suggesting that he or she takes over certain preparations such as researching and choosing a pram, car seat and baby monitor. Finally, it is really important that your partner comes along to as many scans as possible. These are really lovely opportunities to see your growing baby. If you have rented a Doppler monitor it can also be lovely for you both to relax together on a bed and listen to the baby's heartbeat and talk and sing to him together.

Chapter 3: Antenatal care

This chapter is all about the care you receive from the time you tell your doctor or the midwife that you are pregnant, right up to the birth of your baby. You'll have a series of appointments with your family doctor, a midwife, and a doctor who specialises in pregnancy and birth (obstetrician). Depending on your area, check-ups will take place at hospital and your local health clinic and will be carried out by your doctor and/or midwife team. If you have a high-risk pregnancy, you may have all of your appointments at the hospital.

Who's who in my birth team?

There will be a number of different professionals involved in your care. You may not always see the same midwife or doctor at each appointment. You will be assigned to the team of an obstetric consultant but there will be several doctors in his/her team.

General practitioner Your family doctor, or GP, is usually the first person you will tell when you become pregnant. He or she will then talk you through what happens during your pregnancy and help you plan your antenatal care.

Midwife A midwife is someone who is trained to look after mum and baby during a normal pregnancy, labour and birth. She is not a nurse, although many midwives are also trained nurses. You will see a hospital midwife at each visit to the hospital antenatal clinic: for example, for the 20-week anomaly scan. The hospital midwives will look after you through your labour and deliver your baby if all goes smoothly.

Community midwifes will visit you and your baby at home, whether you had a home or hospital birth. You'll probably get to know them during your pregnancy. They are often attached to your family doctor's surgery.

Sonographer A sonographer is a healthcare professional trained to carry out and interpret the ultrasound scans you have during your pregnancy to assess how your baby is growing and developing.

Obstetrician An obstetrician is a doctor who specialises in the care of women during pregnancy, labour and birth. Most low-risk births in the UK are midwife-led and you may only see the obstetrician if your doctor or midwife is particularly concerned about your situation. If your pregnancy is higher risk or requires more scans, your pregnancy will be obstetrician-led (see page 48). An obstetrician will attend complex deliveries, and will always perform Caesarean sections.

Paediatrician This is a doctor who is trained to look after babies and children. A paediatrician may attend your birth if there are concerns or complications. If your baby is born in hospital, a paediatrician will check your baby after the birth.

Health visitor A health visitor is a nurse with a special training in the health of babies, young children and families. About ten days after your baby is born, your health visitor will pop in for a visit and give you your red child-health record book. She will monitor your baby's health and development at home, your doctor's surgery or at the local child health clinic until your child starts school. She will weigh your baby, carry out baby checks with your doctor, give immunisations and advise on any problems you may have.

Doula These are women, usually mums themselves, who have been trained to support women and their families during pregnancy, childbirth and early parenthood. This support is practical and emotional but non-medical in nature. Doulas often say that they 'mother the mother'.

You can have a doula as a birth partner (you can opt for just a doula or she can support you alongside your birth partner) or you can hire a post-natal doula to help you at home with the new baby. She will be rather like a maternity nurse but she will take on the domestic chores and nurture you, so you can focus on bonding with your baby. Contact Doula UK for information.

What is obstetrician-led care?

Most pregnancies are managed by midwife-led programmes, but if you have a higher-risk pregnancy – for example you have health problems such as diabetes, there's a family history of medical problems, or you are carrying more than one baby (see page 104) – you may move to obstetrician-led care. This means that you will always see an obstetrician at the hospital for every appointment. He or she will review your medical notes, arrange for extra scans and if necessary discuss your baby's medical needs before and after the birth. Lots of women who have obstetrician-led care go on to have perfectly healthy babies and straightforward births, so don't automatically panic if you are referred to an obstetrician. Extra scans give everyone advanced notice if your baby becomes unwell and the hospital can arrange to deliver your baby a little earlier if need be.

What antenatal appointments will I have?

Your antenatal appointments can be arranged in your home, at the doctor's surgery, child health clinic or at the hospital antenatal unit. When you tell your doctor or the local midwife that you are pregnant, he or she will discuss your options with you. There are usually around ten appointments for your first child, seven appointments if you've had a baby before. Antenatal appointments will be more frequent if you have a higher-risk pregnancy. Even if you feel fine, don't miss any of your appointments since routine tests and checks will be done that may affect you later in your pregnancy. The appointments will be as follows:

- **5–12 weeks** First appointment.
- **8–12 weeks** Booking-in appointment.
- **10–14 weeks** Combined screening (nuchal scan and blood test).
- **14–20 weeks** Quadruple test if you were too late for combined test.
- **16 weeks** Follow-up of blood and urine results from booking-in appointment and another urine test to look for protein in your urine.
- **18–20 weeks** Anomaly scan.
- **25 weeks** (first pregnancy only) Blood pressure, protein in urine. Bump size should be measuring around 25 cm (10 in) at 25 weeks.

If bigger or smaller you may be referred for an extra scan to assess your baby's growth and amount of amniotic fluid.

- **28 weeks** Blood test to assess maternal iron levels and look for antibodies in the blood to Rhesus factor (If you're rhesus negative, you will be offered an anti-D injection to kill off any antibodies in your blood).
- **31 weeks** (first pregnancy only) Blood pressure and urine protein test. Bump measured again, fundal height from pubic bone to top of fundus should be around 31 cm (12 in) now.
- **32–34 weeks** Repeat scan if 20-week scan showed problems with position of your placenta.
- **34 weeks** Blood pressure and urine protein and bump checked, fundal height should now be 34 cm (13 in). If you're rhesus negative, you may be given a second dose of anti-D to kill off any antibodies in your blood. Discuss birth plan with your midwife or obstetrician.
- **36 weeks** Blood pressure and urine protein and bump checked; fundal height should now be 36 cm (14 in). The position of your baby will be checked; if in breech position you may be offered an appointment to turn your breech baby (see page 101).
- **38 weeks** Blood pressure and urine protein and bump checked; fundal height should now be 38 cm (15 in).
- **40 weeks** (first pregnancy only) Blood pressure and urine protein and bump checked; fundal height should now be 40 cm (16 in).
- **41 weeks** Blood pressure and urine protein; fundal height should be 41 cm (16 ½ in). You will be offered a membrane sweep to help start labour. This is gentler than a fully induced labour (see page 119).
- **Over 42 weeks** – you may need an ultrasound scan to assess the health of your baby, and your baby's heartbeat will need frequent CCG to check the baby isn't in distress and the fetal heartbeats and movements are healthy.

What happens at the first appointment?

You will make this appointment with your GP or midwife as soon as possible when you find out you're pregnant. You will be given advice on nutrition and exercise in pregnancy, the importance of taking folic acid and vitamin D (see page 11), as well as not smoking or drinking alcohol. You will also be advised about the vaccinations, screening and diagnostic tests available to you.

You need to tell your doctor or midwife if you have any particular medical issues such as diabetes, high blood pressure, a family history of abnormalities or inherited diseases, previous premature births or other birthing difficulties; a history of pre-eclampsia,

If you need help with English during at your appointments, your doctor or midwife will have access to materials that will help you get the information you need. Similarly, if you have a physical, hearing or sight impairment, let the team know as they can provide additional support if necessary.

What is the booking appointment?

The booking appointment usually happens when you are eight to 12 weeks pregnant and it can take up to two hours. You will be given information on baby development, nutrition, exercise, breastfeeding classes, maternity and paternity benefits, and planning your birth. Ask as many questions as you like and take your partner or a friend with you.

If you are feeling depressed or anxious, this is really normal, and it's important to bring it up and discuss it. There are all sorts of things the midwives and doctors can do to support you. At this appointment, your midwife will start to enter all your information in your maternity notes book. You need to keep these notes with you at home and bring them to every appointment from now on. You also need to take them with you to any additional doctor/ hospital appointments.

If the booking appointment takes place at the hospital you will probably have your first dating scan at the same time. You will have blood tests to check: your blood group (including whether you are rhesus positive or negative), haemoglobin levels to assess for signs of anaemia, antibodies to rubella (German measles) and the presence of serious diseases such a syphilis, HIV, hepatitis B. In addition the baby's father may be asked to have a blood test so that the team can check for inherited conditions such as sickle-cell anaemia.

What routine appointments should I expect later in pregnancy?

From around 24 weeks into your pregnancy your appointments may become more frequent. If everything is going smoothly, the appointments will be quite short, though. Your midwife or doctor will feel your tummy to check the baby's position, he or she will listen to your baby's heartbeat, measure your uterus to see that everything is growing well, take your blood pressure and check your urine. Findings will be recorded in your notes. You mustn't miss these appointments. High blood pressure or raised blood sugar can sometimes indicate conditions that are potentially serious for you and your baby. If you are having obstetrician-led care you may need more blood tests taken at subsequent antenatal appointments to keep an eye on your iron levels.

You can help by keeping track of number of times a day your baby moves or kicks; if the movements suddenly stop or reduce, you need to tell your doctor straightaway.

Remember you can ask questions about anything: your birth plan, your breastfeeding plan, what will happen during labour, screening tests, your energy levels and moods, domestic violence – anything that affects you and your baby. You may find you've forgotten some of your questions by the time you get to the clinic, so it's a good idea to write them down so you have a list ready at your appointment.

What is a high-risk pregnancy and will it be managed differently?

A birth can be considered high risk for a variety of medical reasons: that there is increased risk to either or both the mum and her baby. All pregnancies have a certain risk, but some carry a higher risk of problems with either the pregnancy or the management of your birth. You are likely to be considered higher risk if you:

- have a history of recurrent miscarriage or stillbirth
- are over 35 years of age
- have type 1 diabetes or develop gestational diabetes
- suffer from long-term (chronic) hypertension or pregnancy-induced hypertension
- develop pre-eclampsia or eclampsia

- smoke, drink heavily or take illegal drugs
- your baby is small for dates (inter-uterine growth retardation)
- you are carrying more than one baby
- your baby is lying in a breech or sideways position (see page 101)
- have had a previous Caesarean delivery and want to try a vaginal birth (VBAC)
- have previously had a pre-term labour
- develop problems with the placenta, uterus, cervix, amniotic fluid, blood and others

If you are deemed to have a high-risk pregnancy, you might be moved from your regular antenatal care team to obstetrician-led care with a high-risk specialist, known as a perinatologist, or a maternal fetal medicine specialist. Your medical team work will with you to decide what's best for your particular situation. It may be that you are high risk only for the pregnancy and not for the birth, in which case you'll be returned to your original team for the delivery.

Will I have more tests if I am high-risk?

You are likely to have more ultrasound scans and, depending on the reason for the high-risk status, your care team will discuss possible tests with you. These include:

- Amniocentesis or chorionic villus sampling to test for abnormalities and some genetic diseases (see page 63).
- Specialist ultrasound on particular area of concern: for example, a Doppler scan to assess blood flow from the placenta to the baby
- Cordocentesis – this tests fetal blood for chromosomal abnormalities. It is carried out when amniocentesis or chorionic villus sampling is inconclusive or if there is a high risk of a genetic defect as this is a higher-risk procedure.
- Biophysical profile – prenatal test on baby's heart rate and general well-being.
- Cervical length measurement – via ultrasound to determine whether you are at risk of a pre-term labour.

• Vaginal swab to check for presence of fetal fibronectin, which can be a sign of pre-term labour. A negative result gives a 95 percent chance that there will be no labour in the next 14 days.

Does the weight and the shape of my bump make a difference?
Weight gain in pregnancy is a combination of the baby, the placenta, increased blood volume, increased breasts and fat deposits (see page 12). Bump shape can vary from woman to woman and from pregnancy to pregnancy. There are small, high bumps; bumps that carry all out front; bumps that don't stick out much but are wide; then everything in between. Your antenatal team will measure your bump regularly to check that it is in the expected range. If it is bigger than expected or smaller than expected you may have extra scans to check that your baby isn't small for dates (inter-uterine growth restriction), or isn't too big (which can be due to gestational diabetes, page 64).

Can I monitor my pregnancy at home?
In recent years there has been an increase in people's ability to monitor their health at home using blood pressure monitoring kits, fetal dopplers that monitor and listen to a baby's heartbeat and phone apps that record physiological measurements such as heart rate.

Some doctors have welcomed this advent of home-based health monitoring – for example, measuring blood pressure at home, rather than occasional blood pressure checks at antenatal appointments. An article in the British Medical Journal reported that eclampsia and pre-eclampsia (see page 66) are not easy to pick up during routine antenatal appointments, concluding that perhaps if more pregnant women monitored their blood pressure at home they would have an early warning of blood pressure increasing, which can be a symptom of pre-eclampsia. Campaigns such as 'count the kicks' are increasingly encouraging women to monitor their baby's movements as a way of picking up any early warning that your baby is stressed or unwell.

If you would like to monitor your blood pressure or your baby's heartbeat, talk to your midwife to make sure that any monitoring you do is done correctly, as incorrect monitoring may give either false reassurance or needless anxiety. Any home monitoring should be in addition to attending your clinic appointments – and not instead of the midwife check-up.

Are there any infections or illnesses that could harm my baby during pregnancy?

There are several infectious diseases that can harm your developing baby (especially in the first trimester); some even result in miscarriage, stillbirth and birth defects. Some vaccinations such as chickenpox and rubella can only be given before pregnancy.

CHICKENPOX AND RUBELLA

If you are planning to start a family and are not sure about what vaccinations and illnesses you have had, you should talk to your doctor about being tested before you try to conceive. Catching chickenpox and or rubella (German measles) in pregnancy can seriously harm your unborn baby. If you had chickenpox as a child you are likely to be immune to it, and if you were given a rubella immunisation at secondary school or are up-to-date with your MMR (measles, mumps and rubella vaccination) you should be protected. It is possible to be vaccinated against both chickenpox and rubella, but this cannot be done while you are trying to get pregnant, or if you are pregnant.

Children with chickenpox (before the 'spots' are visible) are incredibly contagious and even adults with shingles can infect a person with chicken pox. If you are in any doubt, avoid spending time with children or adults with these infectious diseases until you can confirm that you are not at risk of passing on an infection to your developing baby. If you think you have been exposed to these diseases talk to your doctor.

Why am I being offered the vaccinations in pregnancy?

Vaccinations are offered to pregnant women for two main reasons. Some are given to protect a newborn baby from infectious disease in the community. When you are vaccinated, your antibodies will pass across the placenta to your baby so she will be born with increased immunity to the disease. This is enough to protect her until she starts her vaccination programme at eight weeks. Others – for example flu – are given because pregnant women are at significantly greater risk of developing medical complications (for example, pneumonia if they contract flu), especially in the late third trimester because a pregnant woman's immune system is altered during pregnancy to prevent her body from treating the fetus as an invading 'parasite'.

Why would my baby need the whooping cough vaccine?

Pertussis, or whooping cough, is a nasty bacterial infection that causes terrible coughing bouts with a distinctive 'whoop' sound and breathing difficulty. Babies may not have the whoop-sounding cough, but breathing can be seriously impaired and may even stop. Babies are particularly vulnerable and most will need to be treated in hospital as the disease is potentially fatal. The coughing can be so severe even in adults that they may break their ribs coughing.

Even if you were immunised against it as a child, the effect will have worn off so you still need the vaccination to protect you and your new baby. The UK Department of Health is offering all pregnant women a vaccination (currently the 4-in-1 Boostrix IPV, which protects against whooping cough, diphtheria, tetanus and polio) at 28 to 38 weeks to maximise the chances of passing across the potentially life-saving antibodies to the virus and not too late to miss mums who give birth prematurely. There has been an increase in cases of whooping cough since 2012 with over 400 babies catching it; sadly, 14 babies died in this period. It is a terrible disease; our co-founder Dr Rebecca Chicot's younger sister developed it as a newborn baby. She was very ill and caught it because she was too young to have been vaccinated.

Is the whooping cough vaccine safe for pregnant women?

It may feel stressful deciding whether to have vaccinations while you are pregnant, since you feel vulnerable and very protective of your baby. You need to weigh up perceived or real risks to your baby in the womb against risks after she is born. The vaccine doesn't contain 'live' whooping cough so you cannot be infected with it yourself.

It has been in use since 2012 and there's no evidence to suggest that it is unsafe for you or your unborn baby. Similar vaccines have been used in other western countries without evidence of problems. You need to consider the risk to babies of contracting whooping cough before eights weeks of age against potential side effects of the vaccine. The Department of Health currently strongly recommends taking the vaccine to protect your baby.

Why have I been offered the flu vaccine?

Influenza is a highly contagious virus that mutates every winter season. It can make a minority of people very ill and it even kills people who are old or have compromised immune systems (pregnant women) every winter. Pregnant women are at significantly greater risk of developing medical complications if they catch the flu. It can also increase the risk of miscarriage, premature birth and low birth weight. The antibodies in your immune system will also offer your baby increased immunity when she is born.

Since the flu virus mutates each year, the vaccine offers protection to the strain that public health officials think will be the most prevalent that season – so it changes each year. You will be offered the vaccination at the beginning of the flu season (in the UK this is usually from October onwards) – irrespective of the stage of pregnancy. It has been deemed safe to administer to women at any stage in their pregnancy. Annual vaccinations are necessary; immunisation from a previous year does not offer ongoing protection.

What is group B strep?

Also known as GBS, or group B streptococcus, this is a common bacteria carried by up to 30 percent of the population. It can be found inside the vagina of around 25 percent of women. Although it rarely causes any symptoms, in a small minority it infects the baby during labour as she passes through the birth canal. Babies can become very ill and it can be fatal. If you have had a baby who developed a group B strep infection or if you have had a urine infection caused by group B strep you should be offered intravenous antibiotics during labour.

Pregnant women are not routinely screened for group B strep, but it is possible to request a test in the third trimester of pregnancy. Several NHS trusts already offer testing. If your local health trust doesn't offer it you can have it done privately. The Group B Strep Support group is campaigning for all women to be tested.

Your baby is more likely to be infected with group B strep if your labour begins before 37 weeks or if the waters break early before labour begins. If you have a fever in labour or currently have group B strep you baby is more likely to be infected either before labour or during labour.

What scans will I have?

The two main scans during your pregnancy are the dating scan and the fetal-anomaly scan. These scans are painless, and have no known side effects. You don't have to do them if you don't want to, but do discuss the implications of not having them with your antenatal care team. Not only can it be exciting to meet your baby, but these scans can detect problems, which can mean that you are then monitored more often during pregnancy and the birth. If the sonographer can't see everything he or she needs to at each scan, you may be asked in for a further scan a few weeks later.

What happens when I have a scan?

You will probably be advised not to urinate before scans if possible, since a full bladder pushes your womb up and the ultrasound echoes will be able to reach your womb more easily, providing a better image.

If you have an empty bladder the sonographer will ask you to drink a few glasses of water beforehand.

You will be asked to lie down on a special bed beside the scanning device. A cold unscented gel will be spread over your tummy (though some sonographers warm it up first). The sonographer passes a device called a transducer gently over the skin on your bump. The transducer beams a high-frequency sound into your womb. The sound bounces back and the 'echo' creates an image that can be seen on a monitor. Sometimes if the sonographer needs to get a clearer image he or she may press down on your bump or in at the side, which can be slightly uncomfortable, especially with a full bladder. The sonographer will often 'freeze' an image so you can take a printout home.

I have been sent for an early scan. What does this mean?
Your doctor or midwife may recommend an early scan if there are any problems or you have had a previous miscarriage or bleeding. This scan might take place between eight and ten weeks. Sometimes these early scans are carried out using a transvaginal transducer instead of abdominally. This method gives a clearer picture at this early stage of pregnancy. It won't be too uncomfortable and you don't need to keep a full bladder. You can ask for a female sonographer if you prefer.

What is the dating scan?
Towards the end of your first trimester – around 12 weeks into your pregnancy (in reality between 11 and 13 weeks) – you will have the first scan. It is sometimes known as the 'dating scan' since the sonographer can estimate when your baby is due.

The sonographer will 'freeze-frame' images to measure your baby's length (measured from head to bottom, or 'crown to rump' length or CRL), listen to the baby's heartbeat and look at the position of the baby and the placenta (to confirm that it is not ectopic, see page 72). He will also check the number of babies and look for any abnormalities. From the baby's development he can give an estimated due date (EDD), which is particularly important if you want to opt for screening for Down's syndrome (see page 60).

What is an anomaly scan?

Normally given between 18 and 21 weeks, the anomaly scan checks your baby for structural abnormalities. The sonographer can also usually see whether your baby is a girl or boy; be sure to tell him or her if you don't want to know – you will probably be asked.

This time the sonographer can take more measurements. Normally he or she will 'freeze-frame' images to measure: head circumference (HC) abdominal circumference (AC), length of the thigh bone, or femur, (FL), to ensure that your baby is growing well and in proportion.

The sonographer will also examine the structure of important organs such as the heart, brain, umbilical cord, spine, abdominal wall, stomach, kidneys and bladder, and look in detail at the arms, legs, feet and hands. In addition, the sonographer will note the position of the placenta to make sure it is not positioned too close to the cervix. If it is this will be checked again nearer birth as there is an increased risk of blood loss during the birth or premature detachment of the placenta.

The sonographer will calculate how much amniotic fluid surrounds your baby. The amniotic fluid is produced by the baby; too much or too little fluid can indicate fetal distress.

If your sonographer is concerned about growth or anatomy he or she may also carry out a Doppler scan that records the oxygenation levels in the arteries that supply blood to the heart, umbilical cord and brain to make sure your baby's circulation system is working well. If there are any concerns you will be informed of your results in a consultation and may have more scans or treatment.

Later scans

In your third trimester you may be asked in for additional scans if: the placenta looked low in the anomaly scan; you have previously had a very small baby or this baby is very small; you are carrying twins or triplets; if you have high blood pressure or diabetes; or if there are any other concerns. You are unlikely to need a full bladder for these later scans since your baby should be much bigger.

What happens if something appears wrong in the scan?

If the sonographer sees something that concerns him or her, you will be referred to an obstetrician within 24 hours, or a fetal medical specialist, or perinatologist, within three days. The doctor or specialist may then carry out further tests, such as a CVS or amniocentesis (see page 63). If the scan or tests reveal serious problems, talk to the doctors at length to have all your questions and options explored. There are a lot of people at hand to support you through any decisions that need to be made, including midwives, obstetricians, and paediatricians. Make sure you get all the advice you need before making any decisions.

Why have I been offered a combined screening?

At the same time as your dating scan you can also choose to have a 'combined screening' test to assess for the likelihood of you being pregnant with a baby with Down's syndrome, a condition in which a baby is born with an extra chromosome in her body cells. Combined screening includes a nuchal translucency scan and a blood test and is offered between 11 and 14 weeks of pregnancy. The results are compared with the mother's age as the risk is higher in older mums. These tests don't give an actual diagnosis. If your risk is thought to be high you will be offered diagnostic tests to find whether your baby actually does have Downs. Some couples don't want to have these tests and this is entirely their choice.

What happens in a nuchal translucency scan?

This is a screening scan that measures the thickness of the fluid in the nuchal fold at the back of the fetus's neck (it is thicker in a fetus with Down's, possibly due to less efficient circulation system). The test combines the thickness of the fold with your age to assess the statistical chances that the baby has Down's syndrome.

What does the blood test check?

The blood test checks for levels of free beta-hCG (human chorionic gonadotropin) and placenta-associated plasma protein A (PAPP-A) hormones that might indicate the possibility of Down's syndrome. Together these results help to calculate the statistical likelihood of your baby having Down's Syndrome (which is the most common chromosomal disorder).

Are there alternatives to combined screening?

If you miss your chance to have the combined screening test you can have the quadruple test – a blood test that screens for levels of pregnancy hormones hCG (human chorionic gonadotrophin), uE3 (oestriol), AFP (alpha fetoprotein) and inhibin A in the blood as the levels tend to be higher in mothers carrying a baby with Down's syndrome. Alternatively, there is private test that can be done from ten weeks into your pregnancy called non-invasive prenatal screening, or NIPT. Clinics offering the tests claim they are highly accurate at detecting risk for Down's syndrome. The test also looks for Edward's syndrome, Patau syndrome and Turner syndrome. The NHS states that 'further research and evaluation is necessary before these tests are introduced into the NHS, although they are already available in the private sector '.

What tests are offered to diagnose fetal problems?

Around five percent of pregnant women in the UK are offered the choice of an invasive prenatal diagnostic test of their baby. The two main diagnostic tests used during straightforward pregnancies are chorionic villus testing (CVS) done at around 11 to 13 weeks and amniocentesis carried out at 15 to 20 weeks. These tests are used by obstetricians to diagnose Down's syndrome as well as assess whether the fetus could have developed, or is developing, some sort of abnormality or serious health condition such as sickle cell anaemia, thalassaemia, haemophilia, cystic fibrosis, chromosome abnormalities or spina bifida. The results for either test are usually available within a few days. More detailed results take two to three weeks. Be aware that these diagnostic tests do not test for every abnormality.

The tests indicate whether the fetus is a boy or a girl, so if you don't want to know the gender of your baby, tell your obstetrician beforehand.

RISKS ASSOCIATED WITH CVS & AMNIOCENTESIS

These tests involve a number of risks, outlined below, so they are normally offered only to women for whom the risk factor is high. High-risk groups include women over 35, those with a family history of genetic conditions, women whose combined screening presented a high risk, those whose anomaly scan suggested an abnormality, and women with particular individual health histories.

Miscarriage: There is a small (around one to two percent) risk of miscarriage following either test – slightly higher for CVS than amniocentesis. You need to decide whether you think the risk is worth knowing whether or not your baby has a serious abnormality.

Leaking amniotic fluid, needle injury, infection: If you have any leakage that's not urine after the test, any pain, or any infection, seek urgent medical attention.

Inadequate sampling: In fewer than one percent of procedures, the samples removed may not be suitable for testing, and a further procedure may need to be done.

Rhesus sensitisation: Rarely, the tests might result in the baby's blood cells entering the mother's blood stream. If you have Rhesus-negative blood, you'll be given an anti-D injection (see page 49) to prevent you from producing antibodies against your baby's blood cells.

Infection transmission: If you have an infection such as hepatitis C, HIV, or toxoplasmosis, the infection might be transferred to your baby.

What happens during amniocentesis?

Your obstetrician uses a fine needle to extract amniotic fluid from the womb. You may be asked to come to the test with a full bladder, so the scan will produce a better image. When the needle goes in, it might sting slightly. The progress of the needle is guided by ultrasound and once it is in the right place, the sample of amniotic fluid is withdrawn.

You'll need to rest after the procedure and you may experience cramps or small blood spots. If you feel feverish, bleed heavily, have watery fluid (not urine) coming out of your vagina, pain, or contractions, then you should seek urgent medical attention.

The risk of miscarriage is higher the earlier the test is done so it will not be carried out before 15 weeks of pregnancy, but it's usually done between 15 and 20 weeks.

What is chorionic villius sampling?

Also known as CVS, chorionic villius sampling can be used as an alternative to the amniocentesis test (though it does not diagnose spina bifida). The test involves taking a sample of cells from the inside wall of the placenta (the chorionic villi). These cells contain information about the baby's genes. The genetic information in the cells is analysed to see if an abnormal genetic or biochemical condition is present. CVS can usually be carried out earlier than an amniocentesis – around 11 to 13 weeks. It can be performed later if necessary. Again, you may be asked to come for the test with a full bladder so the scan will work better.

CVS may be done transabdominally or via the cervix. For a transabdominal CVS, a needle is inserted through your tummy and guided using an ultrasound scan. A small sample of chorionic villi is extracted via a syringe. This is the usual method, since it's easier to get to the placenta this way. For a transcervical CVS, a thin tube is inserted through your vagina and cervix and guided to the placenta using an ultrasound scan.

There is a one to two percent risk of miscarriage – slightly higher than the risk for an amniocentesis. The risk is slightly higher for a transcervical CVS compared to a transabdominal CVS. If you feel feverish, have heavy bleeding or discharge or contractions, then contact the clinic.

What should we do if there is a problem with the result?

If the tests show a problem, you'll need to discuss the specific results with your obstetrician. Couples who discovered that their baby tested positive for a serious condition often report that being forewarned helped them to plan and begin to come to terms with the result. If it comes to the point where you need to decide whether to continue with the pregnancy, the decision will ultimately be yours, but you can seek advice and support from the specialists available and national support groups.

What is gestational diabetes?

Gestational diabetes, or diabetes during pregnancy, is characterised by higher-than-normal sugar in your blood during pregnancy. A hormone called insulin produced by the pancreas controls the amount of glucose in the blood precisely. However, during pregnancy, some women have higher levels of glucose in their bloodstream and their body is unable to produce enough insulin to process it. Gestational diabetes develops in around one in 20 pregnancies and carries a risk both for mum and baby. In particular your baby will grow bigger than normal due to increased levels of sugar (energy) in the blood going into the placenta.

What causes gestational diabetes?

Gestational diabetes is thought to be caused by a variety of hormones produced by the placenta, which weaken the insulin response in your body. As you approach the third trimester the hormones levels increase and the blood-sugar levels in your body rise. If your pancreas isn't producing enough insulin to counteract the higher sugar/glucose levels, you can develop gestational diabetes.

For some women, gestational diabetes is just something they just get and nobody's really sure why, but for others it can be linked to excessive weight gain or poor diet during pregnancy. Women are more likely to get gestational diabetes if they are overweight and/or over 30. In most women, blood-sugar levels return to normal after the birth. However, there is an increased likelihood of developing type 2 diabetes, so you should be tested for this and/or prediabetes every three years after having your baby. If you had gestational diabetes in one pregnancy, you are more likely to develop it in subsequent pregnancies. In which case you may be tested for it earlier in the pregnancy, at around 16 to 18 weeks.

What are the symptoms?
Many of the symptoms can be mistaken for pregnancy alone, so the blood-sugar screen test helps to confirm the diagnosis. Symptoms of gestational diabetes include:

- extreme exhaustion and irritability – often people just attribute this to the pregnancy
- unusual thirst – again, this can be misinterpreted as a symptom of pregnancy cause just by increased pressure on the bladder, leading to more frequent urination and dehydration
- blurred vision caused by the high sugar levels in the blood damaging the blood vessels in your eyes – this is a common symptom of diabetes in general
- frequent infections, usually of the skin, vagina and bladder – your immune system can be weakened by diabetes, which can lead to more frequent infections
- unexplained weight loss, which happens because the body cells can't metabolise the glucose

How is gestational diabetes diagnosed?
Gestational diabetes can be detected with an oral glucose tolerance test (OGTT), normally when you are between 24 and 28 weeks pregnant. You will be asked to attend the clinic for a morning blood test, before you have eaten breakfast. After the blood test you will be given a glucose drink. Two hours later another blood sample is taken to see how your body is dealing with the glucose in the blood. If your baby appears to be particularly large when it is measured, you will be tested for gestational diabetes immediately. Some women are tested at their first antenatal clinic appointment (8-12 weeks).

What happens if I do have gestational diabetes?

If you are diagnosed with gestational diabetes, you should ensure that your diet is high in fruit and vegetables and whole grains. Choose whole foods that have a low glyceamic index (foods that release glucose into the bloodstream more gradually) such as wholemeal breads and pastas, and other foods that are high in fibre, and avoid sugary drinks, including fruit juice, and sugary foods.

Your baby's growth will be carefully monitored and if she grows very big your obstetrician may suggest inducing the birth from 38 weeks, or delivery by elective Caesarean section (see page 120). Some pregnant women with gestational diabetes will be able to manage the diabetes by eating balanced meals and getting regular exercise. However, some will need to take insulin. You will be shown when and how to check your blood glucose levels.

Why are pre-eclampsia and hypertension risk factors?

Pre-eclampsia – sometimes called 'toxaemia ' – usually develops after the 20th week of pregnancy and is potentially life-threatening for the mother and baby if left untreated. Woman with pre-eclampsia usually have high blood pressure (hypertension), swollen hands and feet and protein in their urine (proteinuria). This is why routine antenatal checks are so important as the antenatal care team monitors you for signs of pregnancy-induced raised blood pressure and protein in your urine.

Pre-eclampsia is quite common, it affects around five percent of pregnancies. By monitoring blood pressure and urine it can usually be detected when it is still mild, which means it can usually be managed until delivery is possible with medication. There is no 'cure' as such, other than delivering the baby; however, if you have moderate or severe pre-eclampsia you will be monitored more closely and may be prescribed blood pressure medication. However, it usually goes away several weeks after the birth. It may mean that your baby needs to be delivered soon after 36 weeks or earlier if the health of the mother or baby demands it. Many women with high blood pressure can hope for a vaginal delivery after 37 weeks. If you develop severe pre-eclampsia it may be necessary to deliver your baby earlier, possibly by Caesarean section.

Are some women at higher risk of pre-eclampsia and hypertension?
You are considered higher risk if you are in one or more of the following categories: this is your first pregnancy; you are in your early teens or aged 40 or over; your last pregnancy was more than ten years ago; you are obese; you have a family history of pre-eclampsia; or you are carrying more than one baby.

In addition, you are at greater risk if: you had high blood pressure before you became pregnant, you had high blood pressure in a previous pregnancy, you have chronic kidney disease, diabetes or a disease that affects the immune system, such as lupus, or you are of African descent.

If you've had pre-eclampsia in one pregnancy, you are more likely to get it in subsequent pregnancies, but if it was mild it is generally less severe the second or third time around.

You might want to discuss using a blood pressure monitor at home during your pregnancy so you can call the antenatal team if your blood pressure climbs rather then waiting for the next antenatal clinic appointment (see page 53).

What other symptoms are there?
Even if you're not in one of the high-risk groups, call your antenatal care team or your doctor straight away if you have any of the following symptoms:

- pain in the upper right part of your abdomen
- swelling of your hands or your face
- dizziness
- sudden weight gain
- blurred vision, or changes in vision
- headaches
- shortness of breath
- anxiety

What causes symphysis pubis dysfunction?

When you are pregnant your body produces a hormone called relaxin, which softens the ligaments that hold the pelvic bones together to allow it to open gently and stretch during labour. Unfortunately for some women they can loosen too much, causing excessive movement in the pelvic joints, especially the pubic symphysis at the front. Symphysis pubis dysfunction, or SPD, can become really painful and seriously curtail mobility. It's really important to limit movements that can aggravate the pain.

SPD cannot be cured but has to be managed during your pregnancy. You may be referred to your local physiotherapy department; some hospitals run SPD clinics for pregnant women.

Is there any treatment that can help?
- Try some core strength exercises that focus on your pelvic floor muscles and abdominal muscles. These are small-movement exercises that tighten and stabilise the area to give extra support to your pelvis and spine. Don't do any sit-ups.
- Wear a support bandage around the pelvis when you are walking. This straps the joint to give it extra stability and support during exercise.
- Exercise in water can help but avoid lots of swimming, especially no breaststroke as the leg kick can really aggravate SPD.
- You should also be given advice on how to make daily activities less painful. Avoid cycling, limit walking, get in and out of bed without spreading your legs each time and keep a pillow between your legs as your sleep. It's really worth making the effort to protect the joints even though it can be very frustrating, especially if you are used to getting lots of exercise.
- Avoid movements and positions that will inflame the area such as crossing your legs, pushing heavy items like vacuum cleaners or shopping trolleys, twisting, and lifting shopping in the supermarket. Ask someone help you pack your shopping and take it to the car for you, or try online grocery deliveries instead.

- If you have severe SPD mention it in your birth plan as birth positions where your legs are very wide apart may be too painful. Discuss active birth positions that don't aggravate it.
- Some women try alternative therapies such as osteopathy and acupuncture. There are no good studies of the effectiveness of these treatments. Osteopathy is not offered on the NHS so make sure any practitioner is qualified to treat pregnant women.

How common is extreme morning sickness?

Around 70 percent of women will experience morning sickness to some degree during their pregnancy. For most women it is an unpleasant, but bearable, experience that recedes by the end of the first trimester (see page 35). Some women, however, experience excessive nausea and vomiting. This is a condition called hyperemesis gravidarum (HG) and affects around one percent of pregnant women. It came to the public's attention more recently when the Duchess of Cambridge suffered with the condition during her pregnancies.

You will know you have HG – not 'normal' morning sickness – if you can't keep any food or drink down, if you are vomiting many times a day (sometimes up to 50 times a day) without respite, if you feel light-headed or dizzy (your blood pressure may lower), and/or if you are losing weight. You may also experience constipation as a result of the dehydration, headaches, periods of incontinence, and/or excessive saliva production.

It's important to seek medical help immediately, since dehydration is a common result and in can affect your health, and that of your baby, as neither of you will be receiving the nutrients you need. There are treatments that might help you such as anti-sickness drugs, vitamins and steroids. If HG is very severe you may need to be admitted to hospital for intravenous fluids and feeding. The earlier you start the treatment, the more likely it is to be effective. If you receive prompt treatment, the good news is that your baby is unlikely to be affected.

What is obstetric cholestasis?

It's quite normal for your skin to feel itchy during pregnancy, but if the itching becomes severe, and there is no rash, it may be an uncommon condition called obstetric cholestasis (OC). This is a potentially serious liver disorder, which sometimes runs in families, and can lead to premature birth and stillbirth. OC is most likely to develop during the last four months of pregnancy and is caused by bile salts leaking into the bloodstream. It affects about one in 150 pregnant women, increasing to about one in 70 for Indian-Asian or Pakistani-Asian women. It is also more common in women who conceived using IVF.

As well as generalised severe itching, the palms of your hands, and/or the soles of your feet can be particularly affected. It may feel worse at night. The condition can't be cured, but the symptoms can be treated. You can use lotions safe for pregnancy such as calamine lotion to help soothe the itching. It is also very important that the condition is monitored medically so you will be transferred to obstetrician-led care. Your obstetrician will want to try to maintain the pregnancy as long as is safe for the baby as prematurity carries risks to your baby. In some cases your baby may need to be delivered early. Women with obstetric cholestasis can develop jaundice, but the good news is that the liver condition and the hideous itching will go after your baby is born. It is important to seek urgent medical advice if you suspect that you may have this condition.

How common is miscarriage?

Miscarriage or the loss of a pregnancy within the first 23 weeks is extremely common.

As many as one in four pregnancies end in miscarriage; most occur in the first 12 weeks. Our society does not acknowledge most miscarriages very seriously, but for a couple it can be devastating.

Why do miscarriages occur and what is done to help?

The great majority of miscarriages are unexplained and the medical profession probably does not always do enough to find out why they happen. There is usually very little treatment possible once a miscarriage is underway – most of them cannot be stopped once the bleeding has started to be anything other than slight. Some women let the womb naturally expel the 'miscarriage' and there is also a 'medical management of miscarriage' that uses tablets and vaginal pessaries to encourage the uterus to contract and expel the tissue inside the uterus. Your obstetrician may do an ultrasound scan to make sure that no tissue remains in the uterus. If it does, then he or she will recommend a hysteroscopy to remove it. This will be done under general anaesthetic, but only as a day case. Most women only need a day to recuperate before returning to work. There is a small risk that the procedure will perforate the uterus and also a small risk that not all the tissue will be removed. If you are in any pain or bleeding continues, call your doctor straightaway.

What does recurrent miscarriage mean?

Recurrent miscarriage is the term used if you have had three or more miscarriages in a row. This happens to around one in 100 women. If this happens to you, you will be referred to an obstetrician/gynaecologist (ask to see someone with a specialism in recurrent miscarriage) who will try to determine the reason for this happening. Miscarriage can be the result of an abnormality, genetic problem, blood problem, hormone issue, your age, disease or injury, or it can just be chance. Many women go on to have babies after several miscarriages.

What are the signs of miscarriage and when should I see my doctor?

There are many different ways for miscarriages to occur. Some women will experience pain, slight or severe; others will have very heavy bleeding. In some cases there are no symptoms at all, and it's only discovered when the woman attends a routine ultrasound scan.

See your doctor immediately if you have bleeding or any of the following:

- Vaginal bleeding. This is the most common sign, but it does not necessarily mean you are having a miscarriage. The bleeding may be brown or red, light to heavy, and may go on over a few days.
- Cramping pains in your lower abdomen.
- Swelling or 'tingling' sensation in the breasts has stopped.
- Discharge of fluid or tissue from your vagina.
- Disappearance of morning sickness.

What is an ectopic pregnancy?

An ectopic pregnancy is one that develops outside the womb, mostly in one of the fallopian tubes. It is potentially be life-threatening as the tubes cannot stretch enough for the embryo to grow and if left untreated the tube can burst. Emergency surgery is needed. Around one in 80 pregnancies is ectopic and once a woman has had one ectopic pregnancy she is much more likely to have another. If you've had an ectopic pregnancy, you can still have a normal pregnancy. Around 66 percent of women who have had an ectopic pregnancy will become pregnant again naturally; others some may need treatment.

What causes ectopic pregnancy?

Like miscarriage, doctors don't always know why someone has an ectopic pregnancy, but risk factors include blocked or narrowed fallopian tubes. The risks are also higher for women over 35 or heavy smokers. But ectopic pregnancy can occur also in women with none of these risk factors.

What are the signs of an ectopic pregnancy?

The signs of an ectopic pregnancy usually start appearing by around week five. If you know you are pregnant and experience any of the following symptoms, call an ambulance or go straight to your local hospital accident and emergency department, as you need urgent medical attention.

- severe pain in the lower abdomen
- feeling dizzy and faint
- possible nausea or constipation
- bleeding from your vagina that is heavier or lighter and often darker in colour than a period
- pain in your shoulders (referred pain)

Chapter 4: Preparing for the birth

Until modern times and the development of modern medicine, home birth was the norm. Research comparing the outcome of home and hospital births has found that for a low-risk pregnancy, a home birth has a lower rate of intervention and a shorter recovery time. In 1959, around 34 percent of women in the UK gave birth at home. Now the rate is around three percent. In the US, some states have rates as low as 0.1 percent. This upsets many people since they believe that the less intervention, the better. And, if all goes well, that's true. Other people think it's safer to be in a hospital where there is back-up if things go wrong. There's a logic to that point of view as well. The debate continues, with heated arguments on both sides. In this chapter we'll try to present the facts in an objective way so you can make an informed choice and prepare for the birth that will suit you and your growing family.

Where should I have my baby?

There are various options available: you can deliver a baby in a hospital maternity unit, a midwife-led birth unit or in the comfort of your home. Assuming neither you nor your baby is at high risk of medical problems, the choice is yours. However, if you are in the high-risk category (see page 51), it's likely you'll be advised to go for the hospital option so that help is at hand immediately in an emergency. You will book in via your family doctor or midwife quite early on in your pregnancy. Rest assured, you can change your mind if you want to – just discuss it with the relevant teams. You may even have to change your mind – for example, if you have chosen a home birth, but your pregnancy becomes more complicated. Your choice may vary between areas; for example, some areas might not be equipped for supporting home births, and that may affect your choice.

In the UK at present 94 percent of women have a hospital delivery. This is a huge change from even relatively recent history when there were many more home births. Although hospital births have become the norm, there are other options for you to consider as well. Some hospitals offer a choice of the midwife-led unit or the labour ward/ delivery suite. The former encourages active birth, water birth, breathing and visualisation techniques to manage the contractions and pain. It is possible to employ all these pain and labour-management strategies in the labour ward too.

In a report released in December 2014, the National Institute of Clinical Excellence (NICE) changed its guidelines on birth location. Professor Mark Baker, NICE's clinical practice director, said: 'Most women are healthy and have straightforward pregnancies and births. Over the years, evidence has emerged which shows that, for this group of women, giving birth in a midwife-led unit instead of a traditional labour ward is a safe option. Research also shows that a home birth is generally safer than hospital for pregnant women at low risk of complications who have given birth before.'

Can I have a home birth?
Around three percent of women choose to give birth at home; it is more common with second babies and subsequent births. Some people worry home births are unsafe, since if anything goes wrong expert help isn't immediately available. However, NICE guidelines published in 2014 reported that for low-risk births, a home birth would be a better option for the mother and as safe for the baby in at least 45 percent of births. The advantage of a home birth is that you are likely to feel more relaxed in your own surroundings and so labour can move along effectively (stress and anxiety can slow or even stop labour in both women and other mammals). The cons are that you will be limited to gas and air for medical pain relief and you will need to be transferred

to hospital if your birth becomes complicated or if there is evidence that your baby is stressed. Mums choose to give birth at home because they:

- Feel that birth is a natural process and not a medical pathology that needs to be treated.
- Feel more comfortable surrounded by their things and family.
- Have other young children they don't want to leave.
- Feel they will have more attention from their midwife.
- Think that they will feel less pain and be able to manage it better in a familiar environment with the assistance of a focused midwife team.
- Have had a unpleasant experience in a hospital before and want to avoid a repetition.

How do I arrange a home birth?

If you would like a home birth it's important to discuss it with your doctor or midwife as it's possible that your particular situation it isn't appropriate; for example, if you have a high-risk pregnancy. These risks are harder to assess for a first baby, but research suggests similar safety rates for home and hospital births, once high-risk/complicated pregnancies are removed from the sample. If it is possible, your choice will be put in your maternity notes. You can book an independent, private midwife, if there is one in your area. She will charge around £2,000-£5,000 to help you right the way through your pregnancy, labour and birth.

It's a good idea for the midwife to visit your home to make sure it's suitable; she'll notice what you simply won't have thought of. Discuss this possibility with her when you first meet. One or two midwives will be with you throughout the labour and birth. If there are any problems or labour is not progressing (and the baby is distressed) you will be transferred to hospital in an ambulance where you will be taken straight to the labour ward

What is a midwife-led birth unit (MLBU)?

A midwife-led birth unit (MLBU) can either be part of a hospital's main maternity unit, or a separate building. These units are a compromise between home and hospital births. They provide the comfort and relaxed surroundings of a home and ready access to medical care of the delivery unit in the adjoining maternity hospital. The rooms look more like a home than a hospital room; there is the option of soft lighting, music, gym balls and birthing pools. Around three percent of pregnant women choose this birthing environment as well.

Your baby is delivered usually by one of the team of the midwives from the hospital. Midwives often choose to work in MLBUs as they feel they can work more naturally with a labouring woman and the woman will have a better birth experience.

Expectant women sometimes choose this option instead of a hospital birth because they feel they have a better chance of being looked after in labour by someone they already know. In addition they feel reassured by the emergency back-up of the hospital. Discuss it with your doctor or midwife during one of your early antenatal appointments. Towards the end of your pregnancy they will assess you to see if your pregnancy is low risk (for example, if your baby is head down and in a good position) and therefore suitable for a MLBU delivery. If you are well you may go home a few hours after the birth. If there are complications, and you need to stay longer, you may be transferred to the postnatal ward in the hospital.

The disadvantage of an MLBU is that won't have immediate access to anaesthetists to administer epidurals or obstetricians or neonatal nurses; the only pain relief available will be gas and air and pethidine (see page 112). Some free-standing birth centres may have cover from these specialists, but most don't. If you need these you will transferred to the delivery unit.

What are the options with a hospital delivery unit?

If you decide to go for a hospital delivery, there may be several local hospitals to choose from. Some offer a choice of a midwife-led unit or the labour ward. If there's a choice of hospitals, visit each one and have a chat to the teams before you decide which best suits your needs, but bear in mind that you will need to travel to the hospital once your labour has begun. Try to talk to local mums to find out where they gave birth and what their experiences were. Some hospitals/areas have a 'team midwifery' system so you'll see someone from the same team each time you visit, and one of the midwives from the team will support you at your delivery.

It is possible to use any pain and labour management strategies in the labour ward, so hospital can be a good option for women who have to be monitored or treated during labour: for instance, those who are having a vaginal birth after Caesarean (VBAC), women whose labour has to be induced, and anyone who has tested positive for group B strep and needs intravenous antibiotics during birth (see page 57). You will need to discuss your birth plan preferences in the context of the extra monitoring you might need, but midwives and obstetricians are keen to support women's birth plan wishes where possible.

One of the advantages of the labour ward is that there is a variety of pain relief available, including epidural, mobile epidural, spinal block and pethidine. However, some midwives and obstetricians would argue that a woman (particularly if in a bed lying on her back) in a delivery suite is more likely to find her labour painful. This can particularly be true for induced births as the process can lead to very intense contractions which some women report feel less productive than natural contractions (see page 95). However, if there is an emergency and you need a forceps delivery or even a Caesarean, the theatre is usually close to the labour ward. If all has gone well you may be sent home after a few hours, once you and your baby have been properly checked. If there are complications after, say, an emergency Caesarean section, you may be kept in for a few days.

How can antenatal classes help me to prepare for the birth and arrival of my baby?

Antenatal classes are designed to help expectant mums and dads prepare for birth, as well as to learn how to look after and feed their babies. There is nothing that can truly prepare you for the birth of your baby, especially if it's your first, but antenatal classes are a great place to start. They help you to understand and think about the birth and what to expect as well as write a birth plan (see page 87). They are also a great way to relax and meet other local couples having a baby around the same time as you.

You may feel it all sounds like common sense and you assume you know most of it already. However, many expectant parents find that they learn a great deal from the courses. Many baby-care skills need to be learned – they are actually not as 'instinctive' as you might imagine. Breastfeeding is a prime example. Some mums find it really easy and natural, but lots need a great deal of guidance and practice before they get the hang of it. Good advice and demonstrations from experts before the birth is vital, since after the birth you'll probably be rather tired and won't have the time or energy to have breastfeeding lessons. If you choose to bottle-feed, you need to know how to safely sterilise bottles to prevent gastroenteritis. You should also learn all the top ways of bonding with your baby. It's not always like in the movies where there's an instantaneous surge of love; knowing the basic techniques of attaching and bonding with your baby can really help. It's also vital to know things like how to recognise signs of trouble – so you can deal with them before they develop further. These might include physical things like mastitis – or emotional difficulties, like postnatal depression. The more you know, the more prepared you'll be, and the better you will cope.

What do classes cover?
If you're having a first baby, classes a great help, since there's so much to learn. For a second or further baby, there are often refresher courses too. Antenatal classes cover a wide range of topics such as:

- different options for where you can give birth e.g., home birth, midwife-led Unit, labour ward
- advice on keeping you healthy and fit
- how to recognise the signs and stages of labour
- when to call the hospital for advice, and to tell them you are in labour
- different ways of giving birth such as active birth, assisted birth, water birth as well as emergency delivery options
- pain-relief options

- breathing techniques (try not to be embarrassed – these can really be helpful, as strange as they sound)
- writing a birth plans
- making a breastfeeding plan
- understanding the emotional journey – including recognising signs of ante- and post-natal depression
- information about helpful support groups
- breathing, relaxation and visualisation techniques to help during pregnancy and birth
- more specific topics like water births, yoga, massage and so on – if you want these you may need to go to a specific course

Where can I find the classes?

The NHS runs free classes, which are normally delivered by midwives and health visitors. Your midwife or doctor should be able to give some information, or ask at the clinic. Other organisations – for example, the National Childbirth Trust (NCT) – will probably have courses in your area; you have to pay for these. Look up the options on the Internet, and/or ask local parents.

As well as general birth preparation and parenting classes there are also a variety of courses run by groups that recommend various birthing techniques. These include hypnobirthing (such as the Mongan method) and active birthing classes (that teach positions and breathing methods to help you give birth to your baby naturally using gravity and relaxed breathing). There are also lots of antenatal yoga and Pilates classes, which help you to prepare physically for the birth of your baby.

Can I take time off work to attend classes?

Women have the right to take time off work to attend antenatal classes – men don't currently have this right, although there is increasing noise for this right to occur. Lots of areas offer classes with at least one evening session so dads can come too – which is a great idea.

When should I book and start?

Book early since classes often get booked up. Classes usually start around eight to ten weeks before your baby is due, when you are around 30 to 32 weeks pregnant. The classes are generally once a week, and the course usually lasts six to eight weeks. If you're expecting twins, start classes at around 24 weeks as there's a higher chance they'll come early. It's worth looking into specialist classes for multiples.

What plans should I make in preparation for the birth?

As the due date approaches it can really feel like time is speeding up so it's a good idea to plan for the practicalities of birth and life with your new baby. It's worth starting to be prepared from about 34 weeks. You can discuss what you need to do when you go into labour in advance with your midwife or doctor – such as when to call them, when to head to hospital and so on. However, there are lots of domestic issues to take care of too.

Alert your birth partner

Have a plan for alerting your birth partner when you go into labour. Don't leave it to chance – he or she might be somewhere their mobile isn't working. Around the time of the due date check that your partner has a mobile phone with him or her at all times. Suggest that he or she checks in with you several times a day in case you are unable to get in touch.

Organise telephone numbers

Put a list of the phone numbers of anyone you might need to alert when you go into labour somewhere obvious – for example, the fridge. A prearranged group text/email address can be helpful as well. You don't want to be spending time looking up people's numbers or making individual calls when trying to concentrate on contractions. You can also save these contact details to an email or an app to share with family and friends.

Know the route to the hospital

If you're driving in, know the route, where to park, which entrance to use and where to go inside and whether you need coins for a meter and so on. If you're going to take a cab, have the number on your fridge list and make sure you have a back-up taxi company as well.

Don't forget your pets

Have a think in advance about whether it might be easier to have your beloved pet stay with friends for a few weeks. It might just be the break you need. If this won't work, make sure there is someone to feed or walk him or her while you are in hospital in labour.

Stock up on essentials

Make sure you've got everything you need for your baby for the first few weeks – so you don't have to think about going shopping. Nappies, clean clothes, cot sheets and blankets, a car seat, a pram, a baby sling, cot or moses basket, nursing bras and pads, bottles and sterilising equipment if you're bottle-feeding and so on. Then also things like lots of frozen meals, staple foods, toiletries, medicines, shampoo, lots of clean pants and socks for everyone. Do anything you can think of that will save you having to do laundry or shopping for a while.

How do I prepare older siblings?

It's very exciting having a new baby coming home but older siblings may not react in the way you hope. It's really wise to talk to them in advance. Discuss the idea of the family getting bigger, and their role in the family. You might think it's helpful to have a baby doll for them to practice cuddling. They'll be a big brother or sister now, and that's a very important part to play. Reassure them they are still absolutely as important as they always have been. If at all possible, have a family member on hand when the new baby comes home, to look after the older ones if they are feeling left out. In fact, if the new baby is asleep try to focus on your older children so they feel they have you back. It can be confusing for young children when their mum leaves for a few days and comes back with a baby that is demanding all your attention;

they need to be reassured that you are still there. A lovely wrapped-up toy or teddy bear hidden in the cupboard to give them a day or two after the new arrival can be very helpful too – or perhaps a specially arranged play date with their favourite friend or aunt. Try and involve them with the new baby as well – helping a little, supervised cuddling, helping choose things for the nursery, giving ideas for the name and so on.

Should I organise help around the house?

Most cultures around the world do a good job of looking after a new mum with a newborn baby. However, in the UK some new parents find themselves isolated and living far away from family. Usually family and friends want to help and be useful so it can really help if you ask for help and plan the support you need before you go into labour.

Have a chore plan for the first few weeks (and months). Discuss it with the family and friends in advance so there won't be any surprises. It might not actually have occurred to them that you may not be able to make lunches, take older kids to school, cook, or clean for a while. If you're very lucky you'll have help for these things for a few weeks or months – a cleaner perhaps, or family and friends dropping by to give you a hand. Try to encourage people to offer to do this for you in advance so you'll have some support. Casseroles in the freezer are a great idea if you have time to do some bulk cooking and freezing – and if people are coming to meet the baby and ask what to bring, suggest a dinner rather than another new baby outfit!

Don't underestimate how much help you will need. All new parents are different, with different family set-ups and different preferences. You will have so much to do looking after the baby that you really need someone to look after you too. Do consider letting your mum (if appropriate) come and stay with you in the early days and weeks. It can be so helpful to have an experienced grandma cuddle the baby while you have a shower or catch up on some sleep. You will be very sleep deprived in the first few days and weeks, in a way that you can't really prepare for, so try to accept help.

What do doulas and maternity nurses do?

If you know that certain offers will cause you more stress than support overall, consider paying for some help. Some women do not have support around them so find a wonderful doula to look after them. Doulas, often mums themselves, are there to look after you and keep the household keep running while you bond with your baby and get used to being a new mum. Doulas can attend your birth too if you want them to. Other women really want a maternity nurse to help them with their baby.

Make sure you meet doulas and maternity nurses well before your due date and check that you get on well with them. New mums sometimes feel almost bullied by some maternity nurses, in-laws or partners who are very prescriptive in the help and baby care they provide. So make sure you are on the same wavelength before you agree to have them help you; then you will be able to trust and accept their support more easily.

What do I need for a hospital or MLBU birth?

You'll need a few things for you and your partner during labour and some items for your hospital stay. Don't forget clothes for your baby too. If you want to hire a TENS machine (see page 112) – you'll need to do this in advance.

What do I put in a hospital bag?

It's a good idea to have a bag ready a few weeks before your due date. The hospital will usually provide the first few nappies and access to breast pumps, but take some nappies with you just in case. You will need:

- paperwork such as ID, your pregnancy medical notes and your birth plan
- high-energy snacks for labour
- hankies/tissues/handwipes
- nightwear
- slippers and/or flipflops (your feet will swell so take a larger size)

- dressing gown or a hoodie if you prefer
- mobile phone and charger updated with all relevant contacts
- your watch
- socks and underwear for a couple of days
- nursing bras and breast pads
- basic toiletries and toothbrush/paste, hair ties and a hairbrush
- some people take antiseptic wipes for the communal bathrooms
- lots of pairs of cheap big pants, or a couple of packs of disposable ones. You will bleed lochia after the birth, so don't pack your favourite underwear.
- sanitary pads
- glasses if you wear them and a case to put them in
- something to relax with – music/book/magazines
- photos of your other children
- notepad and pencil
- something to wear for going home
- something for your baby to wear going home and a blanket
- car seat for your baby; make sure you know how to fit it in the car

Will I need anything to help during labour?

Think about your birth plan: do you have everything you need during the birth? Don't assume that the hospital will have everything you need (check they have lots of gym balls if you are hoping to try active birth positions during labour, or take your own). You may want to have calming music or a visualisation CD or app and a safe massage oil if you would like your birth partner to rub your back during labour. Take some lip salve and eyedrops so you feel comfortable.

Will I need food?

Giving birth to a baby requires a lot of energy and therefore it's really important to keep your energy levels high and continue to eat. When you think you're going to go into labour, have a meal containing lots of quick-release carbohydrates (pasta, bread and rice), which will give you the energy you need to get through. Pack things like high-energy snacks in your hospital bag in case you need an extra hit of energy before giving birth. Think about things you'll actually want to eat, such as a chocolate bar. Also pack a straw as you may be standing up or on all fours and want your birth partner to bring a drink to your lips so you don't have to move.

Is there anything I should prepare for my birth partner?
- a camera or video with charged batteries and extras
- toiletries
- changes of clothes
- something to read/watch
- money and credit cards
- food – if you are in labour at 3am on a Sunday there may be nothing around apart from a snack machine
- change for drinks machines and snack machines

What should I organise for a home birth?
The good news about giving birth at home is that you will have most of the things at hand. You will need plastic sheets to protect your bed and the surrounding floor, and to make a path between your bed and the bathroom (or old newspapers are less slippery and will protect floors too) and some bin bags for dirty linen and rubbish. A bowl or bucket is useful to have by your bed in case you are sick. Have lots of face cloths to help you freshen up throughout labour and a clean warm towel to wrap your baby in when she's born. You might want a hand mirror so you can see your baby's head crowning, and the midwife will need a desk light or torch so that she can check your vagina for tears. Have a bag of toiletries ready and some sanitary towels and big old clean pants (or disposable maternity pants) to wear afterwards. You'll need loose old clothes for you after the birth, all the clothes your baby will need and a pack of nappies.

There are some extra things to think about when you have a home birth and it is a good idea to gather these items well in advance:

Birth pool
It is possible to hire a blow-up birth pool but you will need to discuss this with your midwife and be sure that she is happy to let you go into labour and deliver this way. If you decide to use one, you will probably need to have a clean hose pipe to fill the bath with warm water from your sink Be warned: they take a long, long time to fill up so don't start doing this in the late stages of labour as you will run out of time. A birth pool full of water is very heavy so it is best to have it on your ground floor. Think about how you will empty it and clean it afterwards. If a hired birth pool isn't practical, you can also fill your bath with water for the early stages of labour.

Gym ball
As you won't be confined to a hospital bed you might want to use a gym ball (birthing ball) or a birthing stool to help you get into comfortable positions for labour.

How do I write a birth plan and what is its purpose?
The first stage in preparing a birth plan is to learn about birth and what to expect from books like this, antenatal courses and friends and family. Some couples find that some friends and family are unhelpful; they either terrify them with birth horror stories or by being too prescriptive in what they insist is the only right and proper way to give birth.

Each birth is unique and each labouring woman, baby, birth partner and team is unique. This means that you will need to think about what birth decisions you would prefer and also what you would like to do if changes and decisions need to be made during the birth.

A birth plan helps you get clear in your mind how you want to manage your birth and helps everyone around you on your birth team understand your preferences and help you make the best, possible preparation for your baby's birth.

You can discuss your birth plan with your midwife and she will give you feedback and what will be possible in the unit where you plan to give plan to give birth. For example, you may want a water birth, but the unit may only have one pool – which needs to be booked. If you are having a vaginal birth after a Caesarean what labouring options might be restricted, such as a water birth or active birthing positions? Can you request delayed cord clamping (see page 114). What pain relief would you want to try or which should you avoid (see page 110)?

By discussing your birth plan with your midwife, you will also have the chance to ask questions and find out more about what happens in labour. It also gives your midwife or birth team the chance to get to know you better and understand your feelings and priorities.

It is important that you and your birth partner (and doula if you are planning to have a doula at your birth) fully discuss your birth plan and caveats so that they are able to act as your advocate throughout the labour and birth. This can help if you are tired or 'going into yourself' and don't want to talk to the hospital staff, but trust your birth partner and doula to help you to make the best decisions for your birth. You may not be able to follow the birth plan slavishly, but having had lots of discussion around your birth preferences puts you in the best position to help you have the best birth you can. Once you have written your plan, keep it with your pregnancy notes.

What is a breastfeeding plan?

If you're hoping to breastfeed your baby, what happens after the birth of your baby can have a big impact on increasing the chances of initiating breastfeeding and successfully establishing it. For this reason we really recommend preparing a 'breastfeeding plan' for after the birth plan. You may want to request, for example, that:

- Your baby is placed immediately between your breasts in skin-to-skin contact straight after birth (and not wrapped in blankets).
- The midwife does not cut the cord for around ten minutes (or around one minute following a Caesarean birth)/or until it has stopped pulsating – this is so your baby can go on receiving oxygenated blood and steam cells from the placenta, which lots of experts agree

are beneficial for many reasons, including increased blood flow to the baby, higher levels of red blood cells for the baby, and therefore improved iron levels.

- Tests or assessments of the baby are either done while you cuddle your baby or after you have been in skin-to-skin contact with your baby for over an hour.
- Your baby is offered the breast within the first two hours of birth.
- Unless medically vital, your baby receives no water or formula milk.
- Your baby is offered lots of breastfeeds to get your milk production going and is allowed to feed during the night.

What is the role of a birth partner?

Although birth partners often report feeling useless and powerless during labour they have three very important jobs to do during your birth: they provide emotional support, practical support and they are your advocate. It is important that you discuss this beforehand and decide who will be the best birth partner for you. It may be your partner, it may be your mum, it may be your big sister, it may be your best friend, or it can be a doula – and you can have more than one. Or some women will choose to have both their partner and their mum there so that they can take turns helping, or one of them can get you something to eat while the other one rubs your back. For once in your life, this is all about you.

Throughout history women have given birth with the help and support of other people. In the past the people who attended at births were experienced women who had given birth themselves. More recently in the West, our birth partners have become our husbands, boyfriends, girlfriends and wives. The good news is that they hopefully love you and want to support you but they will need to prepare as best they can if they have never been a birth partner or never given birth themselves. With the help of antenatal classes such as active birth classes, your birth partners can play a deeply important role in the birth of your baby.

What emotional support can be provided?

First and foremost your partner is there to provide emotional support for you through this momentous physical and emotional event. All women who give birth are brave. Whether you give birth by a natural vaginal delivery, an elective Caesarean or an assisted birth you will need the emotional support.

Your partner's support needs to be sensitive and respond to your needs during labour.

Sometimes you will need him or her to be the cheerleader who praises you as you breathe through your contractions or as you lie on your side and stay really still while your spinal block anaesthesia is administered or as you allow a ventouse suction cup to be used to help your baby be delivered.

At other times you will not want to interact with anyone; your partner needs to put his or her ego aside and respond to what you want and need. At other points you might feel be frightened, overwhelmed or exhausted. Again, your birth partner needs to respond to your needs by being your rock, reassuring you that you will be okay and that someone is with you for every contraction, every push, whatever it takes. Even if you do not want to interact with anyone, it's not the same as being alone. A quiet presence can be a huge emotional support.

If you want to use hypnobirthing or visualisation techniques your birth partner can help you to come into a state of deep relaxation and trust or help you to visualise your cervix gently opening and your baby coming out slowly but surely (or whatever visualisations you have been working on before the birth).

What practical support can be given?

When people take on big physical feats such as running marathons or triathlons they have a support team to allow them to get on with the challenge they face and have everything they need to hand. It's the same during the labour and birth of your baby: your birth partner needs to put you first and serve you. He or she might be tired, but you are more tired; your need is greater in this event. A good birth partner is at your side with drinks, food, back rubs, to hold your hair if you are sick, to stroke your face.

We strongly recommend trying to use active birth techniques where possible to make labour as effective and empowering as possible. Your birth partner has a really big role here to help you to get into good comfortable birthing positions that allow gravity to help the baby to be delivered gently and efficiently. You may need your back massaged while you are kneeling on all fours or you may want to have your arms around his or her neck as you bear down in a kneeling position. Make sure you have done classes together so your birth partner knows what he or she needs to do to help you have an effective, active birth.

How can my partner make decisions for me?
Your birth partner should know what your birth plan is and what decisions you would like to make, if possible, during your labour and the birth of your baby. If you are exhausted, in pain or feeling bullied by anyone attending your birth, it is the job of your birth partner to verbalise your wishes so that you can concentrate on the birth (rather than lengthy discussions with midwives). You will also need to discuss and trust your partner to make a decision if something new arises during labour that isn't in your birth plan. So before the birth you need to discuss lots of scenarios and plan ahead. If, for example, the midwife recommends an episiotomy to prevent tearing, what is your preference? Use this book to help guide you through possible scenarios. Preparing and thinking about decisions that might need to be made during labour and birth will take away some of the anxiety. It's like doing first-aid training: you are hoping for the best, preparing for the best but having skills, decisions and practice in place to help you to cope when decisions and events happen during the birth. This should give you the freedom to be in the moment with your birth and go with the flow as you have thought and planned ahead.

Chapter 5: Birth

This chapter looks at the way fashions in birthing have changed over the last century and the implications of these changes. There are pros and cons to giving birth in hospital, and also to giving birth at home. Before you make a choice, try to weigh up each option objectively. If you have a high-risk pregnancy, for example, your midwife or doctors would probably recommend that you deliver your baby in hospital so that his safety is not at risk. Or if your baby is in a breech or transverse position and can't be turned before the birth, your team would certainly recommend that you give birth in hospital as well. This chapter looks at all of your pain-relief options – from breathing techniques and TENS machines to epidurals and everything in between. We'll also tell you about your options if find you need a Caesarean section – it's really good to know about these, especially if you were hoping for a natural birth – since there are ways to simulate a natural birth as far as possible. Delayed cord clamping, skin-to-skin contact, delayed bathing, a breastfeed soon after the birth are all possible with Caesarean deliveries too. Remember, births don't always go to plan. New mums and dads often feel powerless when they're in an operating theatre with a medical team at 3am. If you know what you want, and why, and you'll have a much better chance of getting it.

How has the approach to birth changed?

Women's birth experiences have changed a lot over the last hundred years or so. At the beginning of the 20th century fewer than five percent of women gave birth in hospital.

Before the creation of the National Health Service in the UK after World War II, in 1948 most babies were born at home or sometimes in nursing homes attended by midwives. During the 1950s hospital births became the norm. Women laboured without birth partners and dads were positively excluded. Birth became increasingly 'medicalised' and obstetricians generally managed the care of pregnant and labouring women. Birth was considered a medical condition that needed treatment. This was most extreme in the United States, where women were often anaesthetised during labour and babies delivered with women lying on their back with their legs in stirrups. Assisted birth with forceps delivery was more common, and episiotomy (see page 115) was often routine. Induction of birth was sometimes arranged to make sure that a woman would be in labour when her obstetrician was on duty in the hospital.

By the 1970s, dads were increasingly encouraged to be present at the birth and to take part in antenatal classes. However, even as recently as the 1970s and 1980s in the UK women were routinely given enemas and shaved before birth.

The downside of this obstetrician-led care was that many births were not women-centred or respectful to women and many women were not able to labour happily or effectively in these frightening medicalised environments.

When did a more natural approach begin?
In the 1975 the French obstetrician Frederick Leboyer published a seminal book called *Birth Without Violence*, which promoted the idea of the rights of every baby to be born into a gentle, calm, low-lit environment. He argued that a brightly lit theatre-type environment might suit the obstetrician, but was detrimental to the experience of the mother and baby. His book paved the way for a renaissance in natural labour practices championed by influential obstetricians. Yehoudi Gordon and Professor Nick Fisk have even pioneered the 'natural Caesarean' at West London's Queen Charlotte's and Chelsea Hospital, one of the oldest maternity hospitals in Europe.

What is the approach today?

Try not to listen to the horror stories of previous generations as the birth options for women at that time were very limited and many great grandmothers, grandmothers and even your mother may still have difficult memories of the birth of some of their babies.

Since the early 1990s the National Health Service has sought to offer pregnant women a variety of options, including home birth, midwife-led birth, birth in a hospital labour unit (with the option of pain relief such a epidural), and Caesarean delivery where necessary. Women can choose how they want to labour: for example, an active birth or water birth and so on. The good news is that with a bit of research and planning you can talk to your birth team about achieving a respectful and woman-centred birth experience and enjoy the benefits of readily available medical expertise if your birth becomes high risk or your baby needs medical support after birth. That is not to say that everyone today has the perfect birth that they 'planned', but there is much greater communication and respect between birth teams and expectant couples. There is a greater understanding of how important it is that the care team helps a labouring woman to manage her birth instead of completely taking over.

What is the best way to give birth?

There has been a lot of controversy and changes around the advice given women about the 'best' way to give birth. We live in a time of increased choice and birth plans. The current trend, supported by The Essential Parent Company, is a natural, mother-and-baby-centred approach. Birth is seen as a natural, not a medical, process. The needs of the baby and mother sit at the centre of all decisions – so for example, an induction should not be carried out to suit hospital schedules.

In terms of what is the best birth for you, only by educating yourself and your birth partner(s) can you prepare for the birth you would like. This is not to say that by sheer will you can have the 'perfect' birth, but by understanding how your body might respond to labour you can give yourself the best chance.

Psychologically the best way to give birth is in a place where you feel comfortable, with people that you trust. If you are able to relax and go with the flow you will be better able to avoid anxiety, fear and anger that can make labour and birth more difficult.

Birth is a deeply powerful and personal act and every woman deserves compassion, empathy and to be cherished and supported as she gives birth to her baby. Looking after the labouring woman is the best way to care for the baby being delivered.

No one can completely control their birth experience and that should not be an aim. However, if your are fully prepared physically and emotionally you can help get yourself in the best mental place possible to cope with – and even enjoy – the birth of your baby.

What are the stages of labour?

Every woman's experience of labour will be different, but overall there are three stages of labour. In the first stage your contractions make your cervix gradually open up and efface (dilate and become thinner). This is usually the longest stage and it starts with the latent phase and progresses through to active labour. The second stage is when the baby is born. The third stage is the delivery of the placenta, or afterbirth. Just to complicate things even more, there's also false labour, which you may experience for a few days or even weeks before.

What is false labour?

Before labour begins you may experience false contractions, or Braxton Hicks contractions. These are irregular and don't get closer together as time passes. Changing your activity or resting can make them go away. In comparison real contractions can be irregular in the beginning, but then gradually start to get longer, stronger and closer together. Changing your activity or resting doesn't make them go away.

What does a contraction feel like?

During a contraction your abdomen will feel hard as the muscles of your womb tense up and work to open your cervix gradually, making it wider and thinner (effaced). Your contractions are not under your mental control and are able to push your baby out. As your labour progresses, the contractions will become more intense and closer together and, as your muscles relax after each one, the pain will fade.

What happens in the latent phase?
There are two parts to the latent phase – pre-labour and early labour. In the pre-labour stage you may notice all, or just some, of the following:

- Persistent lower back or abdominal pain, along with cramps and a pre-menstrual feeling.
- Mild contractions – these lengthen over time so you'll know they're real. These help your cervix prepare before it starts to dilate
- Your waters may break; this can also happen before labour starts or later. Your membranes may break with a gush or trickle of amniotic fluid. To prepare for this, you could keep a sanitary towel (not a tampon) handy if you are going out, and put a plastic sheet on your bed.
- A small amount of sticky pink, brown or blood-tinged mucus – the 'show' – coming out of your vagina. This is the plug of mucus in the cervix that helped to seal the uterus during pregnancy. It usually comes away before or in early labour as the cervix starts to open and efface. There should only be a little blood mixed in with the mucus. If you are losing more blood, red and like a period, it may be a sign that something is wrong, so phone your midwife or hospital straight away.
- An upset stomach or diarrhoea.
- Feelings of high emotion or moodiness, usually more so with your first baby.
- Difficulty sleeping.

The symptoms intensify once you are in early labour. You may experience some or all of the following symptoms:

- Contractions intensify, are closer together and longer.
- Your baby begins to drop into position in your pelvis.
- Your appetite may increase.
- Your breathing becomes deeper.

- Walking can be a struggle.
- You need to pee more often.
- Vaginal discharge will increase as more of the 'plug' comes away.
- Mood swings, which can intensify as labour progresses.
- You may have an increase in energy.
- Your waters may break if they have not done so already.

How will I know if I am in active labour?

Active labour will induce the following changes to your body:

- Long and frequent contractions – you probably won't be able to speak during one and will probably be moaning.
- Tiredness.
- Shakiness, chills and/ or sweats caused by a sudden surge in hormones.
- Nausea or being sick, as the body clears its digestive system (again you might have low blood pressure so it's important to ask about this if you are vomiting with each contraction).
- More blood-tinged show .
- Tightness in the throat and chest area.
- Strong pressure in the lower back and rectum feeling like you want to poo; you may start wanting to push.

How much does the cervix need to dilate?

The cervix needs to open about 10 cm (4 in) for a baby to pass through. This is what's called being 'fully dilated'. Contractions at the start of labour help to soften the cervix, so that it gradually opens. The process of softening can take many hours. If you are labouring at night, attempt to get comfortable and relaxed. If you can, try to get some sleep. A warm bath or shower may help you relax. During the day, keep upright and gently active. This helps the baby move down into the pelvis and helps the cervix to dilate.

How will I know I'm in labour?

This is a common question and not as obvious as it sounds. Midwives frequently receive calls from women who are uncertain if they're in early labour or active labour, and who need advice. Hospitals frequently have women turning up expectantly only to find out they're not yet in labour and need to go home again. To save you all the trouble of not knowing, here are some guidelines.

When should I call the midwife?

The midwife will want to know how close together your contractions are, so it's good if you've timed this before calling. The midwife can usually tell by asking you some questions and by the tone of your voice whether you need to go into hospital. The process of softening the cervix can take many hours before you're in what midwives describe as 'established labour' – when your cervix has dilated to more than 3 cm (1 in).

Go to the hospital if you experience any labour symptoms and:

- You are carrying twins or multiples.
- You have any medical problems, for example, group B strep.
- Your first, or previous, labour was super-fast (around two to three hours).
- You are less than 38 weeks pregnant.
- You live a long away from the hospital.
- Your baby is breech or sideways.
- Your baby is moving much less than usual – contact your midwife urgently and count the number of movements you can feel when lying down quietly over a ten-minute period.
- You notice vaginal bleeding – unless it's the tiny little bit associated with the show.

Go straight to the hospital even if you haven't noticed any contractions if:

- Your waters break, as it means the sac around the baby has broken and there's a risk of infection.
- Your baby stops moving altogether.

- You feel a strong urge to push.
- There is bleeding because this can mean your placenta is low and being pushed, or has separated early.
- You are in unbearable pain that stays all the time rather than going in waves.
- Your waters or mucus plug are tinged with yellow, green, or dark brown, because this may indicate the presence of meconium (the baby's first poo), which is an indication your baby may be distressed.
- You have been vomiting for long periods.
- You have a fever, changes in vision, severe headaches, along with abdominal pain (or if you monitor your blood pressure at home and it goes up).

At what point in a normal labour should I go to the hospital?

It does depend on your personal preferences – whether you're super laid back and it's your third or fourth baby and you're happy to wait until the last minute, or super anxious and you'd like to get there early. But (depending on how far you live from the hospital) as a general rule of thumb wait until your contractions are around 5 minutes apart. If possible, give the labour ward a call to let them know you're on your way. The midwife may ask you some questions to check that she agrees that it's the right time to come in. Don't forget to take your notes with you.

What is transition?

As you move from the first stage of labour to the second (delivery) stage, you may experience a strong urge to push. Your midwife will tell you to try not to push until your cervix is fully open and the baby's head can be seen.

What happens in the second stage of labour?

This is the part of labour where the baby moves through the cervix of the womb, down the birth canal and is born. The second stage begins when your cervix is fully open. Your contractions help your baby by pushing him out. The baby's head moves down the vagina until it can be seen. You may feel a burning or stretching sensation as the baby's head crowns and is visible to you (with a mirror), your birth partner and your midwife. When the head is almost ready to come out, the midwife will ask you to stop pushing and to do a couple of quick short breaths, blowing out through your mouth. This is so your baby's head can be born slowly and gently, giving the skin and muscles of your perineum (the area between your vagina and anus) time to stretch without tearing.

The time it takes for the baby to get to this position varies a lot – the descent may be quite quick – or it might take a few hours – especially if it's a first baby. If you feel you're becoming exhausted, tell your midwife and she can check that your baby is okay and guide you in resting between pushes, or you can rest a little without pushing, letting the baby move down on its own. When a contraction finishes, the baby's head may disappear inside again, before emerging again on the next push. Each time it should come out a little further. You can try different positions for pushing until you find one that works best for you.

Once your baby's head is born, most of the hard work is over. With one more gentle push, the body is born quite quickly and easily. You can have your baby lifted straight onto you before the cord is clamped or cut. Lots of skin-to-skin contact has been shown to improve the initiation of breastfeeding in newborn babies.

What happens in the third stage?

Soon after the baby is delivered, your womb begins to contract again and causes the placenta to come out through the vagina. The placenta is expelled naturally by the mother's uterine contractions. Early breastfeeding of your baby can help the mum's body to produce oxytocin, which helps this process along.

When the placenta is delivered the umbilical cord is cut. If you ask for the midwife to wait until the cord stops pulsating before it is cut, this allows the maximum transfer of blood cells, stem cells and immunoglobulins from the placenta to the baby. Look at our section of delayed cord clamping to see if you would like the discuss this as part of your birth plan (see page 114). The midwife will check the placenta to make sure all of it has been delivered and none has been left inside.

What is a managed third stage?

Sometimes the mother is offered an injection of an oxytocin-like drug – syntocinin or syntometrine – after the baby is born to contract the uterus and encourage the delivery of the placenta. Managed third stage is sometimes recommended for high-risk births to reduce the risk of bleeding in the mum at the birth (although there is also increased chance of bleeding after the birth due to retained placenta).

There are pros and cons -- some women find these drugs make them feel sick and cause headache – so it's worth investigating your hospital's practice and adding your preference to your birth plan. Discuss it with the team in the early stages of labour as you may be too tired or focusing on your lovely new baby when you get to the third stage. The injection is routine in some hospitals too so don't assume you will have a 'natural' third stage.

Does a baby's position make a difference to labour?

The 'presentation' of your baby means how you baby is lying in your womb. Up to about 30 weeks, your baby will be moving around a lot – which you will probably feel. Then he will usually settle into a head-down position, ready to be born head-first. This is known as 'vertex' or 'cephalic' position – all these words meaning the top of the head. Usually a baby in the vertex or head-down position has his face towards his mum's back (occiput anterior) so that he can move more easily down the birth canal. There are other ways your baby may present that you should be aware of, since some of them make a vaginal delivery more difficult or risky and may require a Caesarean delivery.

What is a breech presentation?

A breech presentation – when your baby is positioned bottom or feet first – is the most common position other than head-first presentation. This occurs in around three percent of pregnancies. Your obstetrician and midwife will probably arrange an ultrasound for you before advising on the safest way for your baby to be delivered. It might be a vaginal birth, or it might be a Caesarean section, depending on your situation. If you do opt for a vaginal birth, it will be a little more complicated than a normal, head first delivery as a baby starts to breathe when he feels air on his chest; if the head is last out, he may start breathing too soon. An epidural will usually be recommended. Forceps are often also needed to deliver the baby's head. In some hospitals, you will be offered the option of an external cephalic version at around 37 weeks (see below).

Breech presentation is more likely if the labour starts prematurely or if you have fibroids, excessive amniotic fluid, more than one baby, placenta praevia (see below) or an abnormally shaped uterus. In the past, breech deliveries were a relatively common part of midwife experience. Midwives today have less experience of assisting the vaginal delivery of a breech baby.

Can a breech baby be turned?

It can sometimes be possible for your obstetrician to move your baby into a head-first birthing position by applying pressure in a particular position on your bump. This is called an external cephalic version. It can be a bit uncomfortable, but doesn't usually hurt. It works around 50 percent of the time, and your baby will usually stay in the head-down position after being turned. This option is only offered after 37 weeks (if it's done earlier there is a chance that you might go into premature labour) and it can only be done if there is enough amniotic fluid around the baby to cushion the turn. There is also a small risk of separating the placenta, or complication with the umbilical cord, so the procedure is undertaken in hospital where you and the baby can be monitored, there is ultrasound and there's emergency back-up if necessary. If the external cephalic version doesn't work, your obstetrician will discuss the alternatives with you – almost always involving a hospital birth, and very possibly a planned Caesarean section.

Can alternative therapies help turn a breech baby?

You probably know someone who was delivered vaginally even though they were in breech position, or who has tried alternative therapies.

Unsurprisingly, many traditional and alternative therapists have tried to turn babies using anything from Chinese medicine (acupuncturists using moxibustion) to yoga.

There have been a number of studies designed to see if these techniques work, but such studies are generally too small or lacking in rigour. We follow Department of Health guidelines and support only evidence-based therapies so cannot recommend the safety or efficacy of therapies that haven't been assessed adequately. If you have a breech baby, ask your obstetrician for advice.

What is a back-to-back presentation?

In the back-to-back position, known as occiput posterior, the baby's back is against your back, with his face looking outwards. You may have what's called a back-to-back labour, which is often longer and can be more painful as contractions tend to push baby against your back rather than down towards the cervix. Sometimes these babies may rotate during labour to the easier occiput anterior position, but some don't. If the baby doesn't turn, you are more likely to need an assisted delivery.

My baby is transverse. What does that mean?

Many babies lie sideways early in the pregnancy and turn head-down for the last trimester. A few will stay sideways, which can present a risk during the birth since the umbilical cord can sometimes come out of the womb before the baby. If this happens ('umbilical cord prolapse') the baby then needs to be delivered very fast he will no longer be supplied with oxygen and may die. Sometimes it's possible to turn the baby before the birth – you can discuss this for your particular case with your obstetrician. It's almost impossible for a transverse baby to come out naturally, so the usual option is an elective Caesarean section. Your baby is in a sideways position, usually with the shoulders or back over your cervix. If the shoulder is presenting first, this position is sometimes called the 'shoulder' position.

The risk of a transverse position increases if you go into labour prematurely, if you have placenta praevia or if you have had many babies.

What happens if the placenta is very low?

The placenta develops wherever the fertilised egg embeds in your uterus. If this happens in the lower part of the uterus, the placenta will develop in a low-lying position. This often happens and the placenta will then gradually migrate up the uterus as the pregnancy progresses and the uterus expands with your growing baby. If the placenta is still lying low after 20 weeks (this can be seen on your anomaly scan), it's called placenta praevia. This occurs to some degree in around 1 in 200 women. Repeated scans will be suggested to monitor its position.

If the placenta is still covering your cervix near your due date, your baby's exit route through your vagina could be blocked. The placenta may be partly covering your cervix (partial placenta praevia) or completely covering it (major placenta praevia). In either case your baby will need to be born by planned Caesarean section. Sometimes placenta praevia is the reason your baby might be in a breech or traverse position.

How are twins and multiples delivered?

The vast majority of twin and multiple pregnancies have obstetrician-led care and a hospital birth due to the increased levels of complications both in pregnancy and birth – 40 percent of one or both twins need to be cared for in NICU or SCBU after they are born (see page 134). Twin births are generally planned to be delivered before 38 weeks to reduce the risk of stillbirth. If you would like to give birth in a midwife-led unit or at home you will need to speak to your birth team to discuss what your options are. Around 40 percent of twins are delivered vaginally and 60 percent by Caesarean section, so discuss your preferences and how the pregnancy is going with your birth team. For example, the delivery method may depend on whether or not the twins share a placenta or have one each.

In a vaginal delivery the first baby is born and then your midwife or obstetrician will check the position of the second baby by feeling your tummy and doing a vaginal examination. The team may check the babies' positions during labour using an ultrasound scan. If the second baby is in a good position for birth, it should be born soon after the first, as the cervix is already fully dilated (less than 20 minutes later on average). If your contractions stop after the birth of the first baby, hormones may be added to the drip to restart them.

Triplets or more are usually delivered by a planned Caesarean section. However, if all the babies are head down, and the mother and babies are all healthy, vaginal delivery may be considered. That said, vaginal delivery of three babies is complicated since all babies may need to be monitored individually, so extra equipment and staff will be needed. An epidural will probably be recommended since the obstetrician may need to reach inside to help position the babies and this can hurt.

What is a natural birth?

A natural birth generally describes a vaginal delivery where the woman labours with support from her midwife and birth partner, doesn't have any pain relief and there is no medical assistance during the actual delivery. A natural birth can take place in water, squatting, kneeling on all fours or even on a bed. After the birth, the baby is passed straight to the mother and placed on her chest. If the birth is in a pool the mother may bring her baby out of the water herself.

The cord will not be cut for several minutes until it has stopped pulsating to maximise the blood that is passed from the placenta to the baby. You will not have a managed third stage, either. Instead, the placenta will be expelled naturally by contractions while the mother cuddles or breastfeeds her baby. After a natural birth the mum and baby are generally left in quiet and low lights.

Woman can feel very disappointed and like a failure if they wanted to have a natural delivery but needed help. It's important not to feel like this. Remember that the ultimate goal of any decisions around labour and birth is your safety and that of your baby, so don't be hard on yourself. There are lots of chance factors during labour and every birth is a unique event.

What is a water birth?

Water can play a wonderful role in birth, whether during labour or for the birth itself. Most midwife-led units and labour wards offer water birth as a birth option, but you may need to book it or tell the unit/ward this is your preference when you call to say your are coming in. You can hire a pool for a home birth. Being in warm, deep water allows women to get in lots of comfortable positions both to cope with contractions during labour and deliver their baby. It has been argued that a water birth makes the transition from the warm, watery environment of the womb to the outside world more gentle for your baby too. Babies can be safely born underwater without the risk of drowning as they receive their oxygen via the umbilical cord until they take their first breath of air. Due to the 'dive reflex' a baby does not take its breath of air until its face comes into contact with air – an amazing instinct to witness. Midwives have reported that babies born in water are calmer and cry less than other babies.

If you have a low-risk pregnancy your antenatal team should support you in wanting to use a birthing pool. During a water birth you can only have gas and air for pain relief – you can't have pethidine or an epidural. However, provided you are on a labour ward, if you are struggling to cope you can ask to come out of the water and have pain relief.

What is active birthing?

Active birthing seeks to use gravity and your body movements to help with the birth of your baby. The angle of the birth canal means that when you are lying down you effectively have to push your baby 'uphill' to be deliver her. By being in a more upright position, gravity helps your baby move down through the birth canal. You can have an active birth in a pool too. Good positions for active birth include:

- standing and swaying your hips
- sitting on a birthing ball
- sitting on a chair facing backwards, so you can hold the back of the chair and bear down

- kneeling on all fours
- crouching, holding onto something or on a small birthing stool

Active birth is a very woman-centred approach to birth, which seeks to empower and encourage pregnant women to get in touch with their own bodies and to keep active during labour. It works with a woman's body and mind to bring their babies safely and gently into the world using the natural positions, and the techniques teach pregnant women to think and respond to labour with a positive mind-set. Relaxation and visualisation techniques help cope with the contractions.

How can my birth partner help?

Your birth partner can work with you during an active birth to help you get into comfortable and effective positions. You might find that it helps to stand with your arms over your birth partner's shoulders, or if you are sitting on a birthing ball or chair you birth partner can massage your back to help ease any back pain.

How do hypnobirthing and hypnotherapy work?

Hypnobirthing, sometimes known as the Mongan method, is a deep-relaxation technique in which you take yourself into a state of hypnosis during labour (or your birth partner can hypnotise you). The theory is that anxiety and stress slow down and disrupt the natural process of labour. Indeed, it is well-documented that labour can completely stop in both animals and labouring women during high stress.

There is also evidence that our pain perception is affected by anxiety levels; anxious people feel more pain from the same stimulus than relaxed people. If you are interested in using hypnobirthing it should be part of your birth plan. You will need to attend a special course with your birth partner to learn the hypnosis techniques before you go into labour.

Hypnotherapy is used before the birth in the antenatal period to embed positive messages and feelings about the birth into your brain. The idea is that when you go into labour you will respond to the birthing process more calmly and embrace it. If you would like to try antenatal hypnotherapy you will need to find a therapist who specialises in antenatal hypnotherapy and book in several sessions before your baby is due.

What is a high-risk birth?

A high-risk pregnancy is one associated with a condition that puts the baby or the mum at a higher risk of complications. However, this does not necessarily mean you'll have a high-risk delivery. A high-risk birth is one where there is a greater chance of complications for the delivery process – including breech and premature birth. A birth can be considered high risk for a variety of medical reasons: that increased risk to the health and well-being of either or both the mum and her baby. All pregnancies carry a certain amount of risk, but some have more risk factors than others, including:

- woman who have had recurrent miscarriage
- small-for-dates baby (inter-uterine growth retardation)
- women who are carrying more than one baby
- some older mums (over 35) as there's a higher chance of miscarriage, high blood pressure, pre-eclampsia, placenta praevia and diabetes
- mums who smoke, drink heavily or take illegal drugs
- babies in a breech or transverse position
- vaginal birth after Caesarean
- women with gestational diabetes or type 1 diabetes
- history of pre-term labour
- women with chronic or pregnancy-induced hypertension
- women with pre-eclampsia/eclampsia
- problems with the placenta, uterus, cervix, amniotic fluid, blood and others

How are high-risk births managed?

In a high-risk birth you will be kept on the delivery ward and monitored carefully with continuous electronic fetal monitoring (EFM). Two belts are placed around your bump. One measures your contractions and the other one monitors and records the baby's heart rate. If your baby is in distress this can show up on the monitor and may mean that you need an assisted birth or even a Caesarean. It is not always easy to interpret EFM readings, so your birth team might err on the side of caution and intervene as soon as they see any signs of distress in your baby or you.

It can be hard to labour comfortably and effectively with EFM so you might discuss intermittent testing or ask whether you can sit on a gym ball while the monitors are attached. If your waters have broken the midwife may attach small clip monitor to baby's head instead.

I had a Caesarean for my first child. Can I have a vaginal delivery?

Between 70 to 90 percent of women who have had previous Caesareans go on to deliver vaginally successfully. The good news is that success rates with vaginal birth after Caesarean, known as VBAC, are documented as being similar to ordinary vaginal deliveries. Statistically, the risk to mother and baby of a VBAC delivery is slightly lower overall compared with having another Caesarean section. This is because Caesareans carry their own risks in terms of abdominal surgery, blood loss and other complications.

However, a VBAC delivery is not risk-free, either (no birth is), and a small percentage of deliveries – less than 0.5 percent – will suffer a uterine rupture. This occurs when the uterus splits along the scar line of the previous Caesarean as it contracts. Uterine rupture can happen with women who haven't ever had a Caesarean, but they are very rare. If your scar is a classic lower horizontal scar most obstetricians and midwives should support you in trying to deliver your baby vaginally. If your scar is vertical, there are other complications or your antenatal team may recommend an elective Caesarean instead.

Are there any other benefits of VBAC?
One increasingly apparent benefit of a VBAC delivery is that when your baby is delivered through the birth canal his skin and intestines are naturally colonised with your friendly bacteria. Babies born by

Caesarean section have significantly different gut flora seven years after birth. This lack of natural colonisation of vitally important; friendly bacteria has been implicated in the increased levels of coeliac disease and diabetes in children born by Caesarean. In the future it might be recommended that babies are artificially colonised with their mum's vaginal flora after a Caesarean delivery by anointing them with vaginal secretions at birth.

What are the different pain-relief options?

There are many different pain-relief options available to you. Every labouring woman has her own unique experience of birth; some find they manage with no pain relief and others need help – there is no right or wrong approach. Learn about labour, birth and coping with contractions and pain. Don't assume that what your friends say was right for them will necessarily suit you or your particular labour experience. You might have a very straightforward birth yet still feel the need for an epidural. Similarly you may have an induced birth or your baby is presenting 'back to back' and you may not be able to cope via breathing techniques alone. Pregnant women can come under a lot of pressure from other mothers who tell you that you will be failing if you don't have a natural birth with no pain relief, to those who insist that an epidural is the only way to give birth. It is important to protect yourself from bullying or evangelical attitudes, especially if they don't fit in with your preferences.

At the same time keep an open mind – you might need more or less pain relief than you first thought, a chosen option might not suit you, or the delivery team might need to suggest that you change for a particular reason. Be kind to yourself.

Try to do some research and ask advice from friends or midwives in advance, then write down your thoughts in your birthing plan. Discuss these options with whoever's going to be with you for the birth, so they can discuss these with birth team on your behalf if necessary. Go to your antenatal classes, read about your options and ask questions, so you know what to expect. That way you'll feel more in control. Active birthing classes can really help you to trust and use your body in the early stages of labour to help labour progress.

At the start of the labour, it's good if you try to do as much as you can naturally. The midwives will encourage you to move around – try to if you can; gravity is a great force and will help move things along. There are several natural methods of pain relief: breathing, visualisation and water. For some women these are enough to see them through. There are further pain-relief options available if not.

Breathing techniques

The idea is to take a deep breath at the beginning of a contraction – breathe in through your nose and out through your mouth, keeping your mouth soft and slightly open. Try to keep a rhythm going – with a regular even in-breath and out-breath – don't worry if it's slow or fast, just try to keep them the same. You might try to do an extended out-breath during a contraction to prevent yourself from hyperventilating or panicking. Practice breathing and relaxation methods before the birth, so you can use them through the labour. You can do this in an antenatal class, or by asking friends or your midwife. Relaxed breathing helps manage pain and anxiety.

Visualisation

Visualisation can help you to manage pain and anxiety psychologically; anxiety can produce a fight or flight response, which can slow down or stop labour. Try to visualise your body giving birth to your baby; you might visualise your cervix opening like a flower or the baby easing through your birth canal. This can lower your anxieties and help you to labour more effectively and positively.

Water for pain relief

Baths are a lovely pain relief during labour. Being in water during labour can be very relaxing and can help with the contractions. You are also weightless, which gives you the freedom to move into different comfortable positions without getting tired from holding them.

TENS machine

TENS stands for transcutaneous electrical nerve stimulation. These machines are supposed to work by stimulating the body's own natural painkillers, called endorphins. They are also believed to reduce the number of pain signals sent to the brain via the spinal cord. Ask in advance whether your hospital has them. If not you'll need to hire one. It is useful to have it at home for a while before the birth so that you can learn how to use it.

TENS can be relaxing during the early stages of labour, but there's no evidence of it being effective during the later, active stages of labour. You can't use a TENS machine in water.

Gas and air (entonox) or laughing gas

This is a mix of oxygen and nitrous oxide gas given through a mouthpiece. You breathe it in just as a contraction begins and it takes about 20 seconds to work. You're in control – you hold the mouthpiece and breathe in as much or little as you need. You can practise using the mouthpiece in advance if you want to at an antenatal class or ask your midwife. There are no known harmful side effects. It can make some people feel sick, sleepy or light-headed.

It might not give you enough pain relief – in which case you can use one of the other methods. Your midwife will bring gas and air to a home birth.

Pethidine and other pain-relief drugs

The aim of these drugs is to relax you to help you cope with labour. They are intramuscular drugs that are injected into your thigh or bottom. Pethidine is the most commonly used, but it could also be diamorphine or meptazinol. The drugs usually take about 20 minutes to work, then last around two to four hours. Some women say the drugs make them feel sick. They can make it very difficult to push if the effect hasn't worn off by the time the baby is ready to be born. A half-dose to start with can be a good idea for this reason. If the drugs are given too close to the time of birth, they might affect the baby's breathing and can interfere with the baby's first feed.

Epidural (or spinal anaesthesia)

An epidural is an anaesthetic, usually given to the mother in bed, that can only be given if you are in a hospital as it must be administered by an anaesthetist. Mobile epidurals (a low-dose epidural), which can allow you to use active birth positions, are available in some hospitals. The anaesthetist numbs a small area of your back with a local anesthetic and then introduces a needle into your spine. A tube goes through the needle and the anaesthetic is passed though the tube. The tube will be taped to your back and the epidural can be topped up as necessary. An epidural takes about ten minutes to set up, and another ten or 15 minutes before it starts working; it may need adjusting afterwards. Unless you have a mobile epidural you will not be able to move around. Your contractions and the baby's heart rate will need to be constantly monitored using an EFM (see page 108). You will either have two belts around your abdomen or possibly a clip monitor attached to the baby's head.

An epidural usually gives complete pain relief, although around 12 percent of women say they need another form of pain relief as well. An epidural can prolong the second stage of labour. Since you won't be able to feel your contractions, the midwife will have to tell you when to push. In addition, as your pushing won't be as effective, ventouse or forceps may be needed to get the baby's head delivered (see pages 116-117). However, it may be possible to request that the epidural level is reduced towards the end so you can push the baby out naturally. On rare occasions, your blood pressure may drop, but this is unlikely and will be monitored.

Alternative methods of pain relief

There are many alternative methods of pain relief, including treatments such as acupuncture and aromatherapy. You can discuss these with your midwife or a specialist in advance if you are interested. There is little peer-reviewed evidence that these provide effective pain relief, although this may be because the assessments just haven't been done. Further advice on these is available from the Institute for Complementary and Natural Medicine.

What are the dangers of going overdue?

Babies that are overdue are at increased risk of stillbirth as the placenta will start to fail. It is hard to know the exact risks because the vast majority of women have their birth induced by 42 weeks (and sometimes even before that). However, induction is not something to be taken lightly as it can have profound affects on the birth experience for mums and babies (see page 118). You and your doctor may want to discuss the advantages and disadvantages of waiting to go into labour naturally versus induction. An induced labour is statistically more likely to end in a Caesarean section.

If you are confident that your baby's due date is accurate and the length of the pregnancy matches your other pregnancies you could ask for more Doppler scans to assess the efficiency of the placenta.

Is there a natural way to stimulate labour if I am overdue?

There are some non-medical techniques that women use to help encourage natural labour. They include eating foods such as pineapple or spicy foods. There's very little evidence to suggest these will actually induce labour, and while something like pineapple may have a small effect you'd have to have as much as seven pineapples in one sitting for any effect. Raspberry-leaf tea has been documented to make the uterus contract more effectively, but it's not proven to induce labour. In the last century women were asked to drink a disgusting cocktail of castor oil and orange juice as this worked like an enema, which was thought to encourage contractions to begin. You can trigger production of the labour hormone prolactin by stimulating your nipples – this also helps milk production.

Should cord-cutting be delayed?

Once your baby's cord is clamped no more blood passes from the placenta into the baby. If it is not clamped immediately, the red blood cells continue to transfer to the baby until the cord has stopped pulsating. There is also evidence that women are less likely to haemorrhage if clamping is delayed. NICE guidelines recommend delaying the cutting of the cord to allow all the fetal blood to move across into the baby's body, which is important for oxygenation and iron stores and is what happens in nature.

Talk to your birth team if you would like to delay the clamping and cutting of the cord. It is generally possible in low-risk births, even some Caesarean births. The delay might range from one to ten minutes (in a birth where the mother has delivered the placenta naturally). If you have a managed third stage (where the delivery of the placenta and the contraction of the uterus are sped up with the administration of an oxytocin-like injection) you can still request a delay to cord-clamping. With delayed cord-clamping there is an increased likelihood of jaundice that might require phototherapy.

Benefits for premature babies Delaying cord-clamping was first encouraged for babies born prematurely. As well as allowing more red blood cells to pass to the baby (which reduces anaemia), it is also thought that immunoglobulins and stem cells pass into the baby, which could improve his body's ability to repair organs.

Benefits in full-term babies After birth the artery in the umbilical cord keeps 'pumping' and if it continues babies may benefit with a 30 percent higher blood volume, a higher red blood cell count and therefore higher iron levels.

What is an episiotomy?

An episiotomy is a small asymmetric surgical cut into the perineum (between the vagina and the anus) to allow the baby more space to come out. The skin of the perineum usually stretches well, but it may tear. An episiotomy can sometimes speed up delivery if a baby or labouring woman is in distress, but it is also sometimes used to prevent a perineal tear, which can occur, for example, when the head and shoulders are presenting at the same time. You may need an episiotomy if you are having a forceps or ventouse delivery.

Episiotomies are controversial and were overused in the past. Sometimes women have felt that an episiotomy has been carried out on them without a full explanation of why it was needed. However, sometimes episiotomies do prevent bad tearing.

How is an episiotomy done?

Before the cut is made you will be given a local anaesthetic so it should not hurt. After your baby and placenta is delivered an episiotomy will need to be stitched. The repair may be done in the delivery room or you may be taken to the operating theatre. If you need more local anaesthetic ask your midwife or obstetrician. Recovery from an episiotomy is longer than small stage-one tears, but quicker than more serious stage-two or -three tears (see page 124).

Can I prevent an episiotomy?

Sometimes an episiotomy is necessary, but you can reduce your chances of needing one by preparing the perineal area to stretch in the run up to the birth. Give yourself perineal massages: using a safe carrier oil, gently insert your thumb into your vagina and stretch the back wall of your vagina around the perineum. Breathing and relaxation techniques and active birthing can help your labour to progress more easily as gravity and movement help the baby to progress through the birth canal.

What happens in a forceps delivery?

Forceps look a little like two metal salad spoons. They are inserted into the vagina, one at a time, on either side of the baby's head, then connected. Your obstetrician will then use the forceps to gently turn and pull the baby at the same time as you push during a contraction. As your baby's head is about to crown an episiotomy is performed.

Forceps delivery is more effective than a ventouse delivery, see below, but there is a greater risk of damage to your vaginal area and your baby may have bruises on his head.

Why might a birth need assistance?

The aim of an assisted birth is to speed up and help you and your baby complete the second stage of labour safely. Your midwife or birth team may want to discuss trying to assist the delivery if they notice signs that your baby is in distress – she may be unwell or may not be coping well with the demands of labour. Likewise it may be necessary because your labour isn't progressing. Although an assisted delivery is generally not what a woman would choose, it can and does save the lives of babies and mothers.

It is not always possible to avoid an assisted delivery, but it's a good idea if you and your partner fully understand the options available to you. You will be less likely to require an assisted delivery if you labour with a very supportive birth partner (especially a doula, who will have lots of experience of helping women to cope with contractions and use breathing, relaxation and active birthing positions to help labour along). This in turn can also reduce the need for epidural pain relief – women are more likely to need an assisted delivery after an epidural. That being said, an epidural may also be necessary because the labour is more difficult and painful, so needs more assistance. It's not a simple causal relationship.

Your feet will probably need to be in stirrups or supports on either side of the table/bed for a forceps or ventouse delivery. They are often done in an operating theatre as if it fails the doctor may need to proceed quickly to a Caesarean section.

What happens in a ventouse delivery?

Either an obstetrician or a midwife with special training will apply a special suction cup, or ventouse, to your baby's head. The vacuum created helps to pull out the baby during a contraction.

The cup can cause swelling and bruising to your baby's head (called a cephalohaematoma) or damage to your baby's retina. Ventouse is usually only attempted during three contractions. If it is unsuccessful, the suction cup will be removed. You don't always need an episiotomy for a ventouse delivery.

What happens if the forceps or ventouse fails?

If these methods of assisted delivery haven't worked your baby may need to be delivered by emergency Caesarean section. If there is time you will be given a spinal block or epidural (if you already have one it can be topped up). In some emergency situations you may be given a general anaesthetic as it is faster-acting, allowing your baby to be delivered very quickly (see page 122).

Can I hold my baby after an assisted delivery?

After your baby is born you can still ask to have skin-to-skin contact with her, and for the cord-clamping to be delayed, provided your baby doesn't needs medical treatment straightaway. Your partner needs to know that this is still part of your preferred birth plan, since the assisted delivery may be unexpected and your birth partner may have to discuss your preferences with the team in the operating theatre. It is also worth noting that a catheter (a tube that drains urine from your bladder) might be needed for 24 hours after either a ventouse or a forceps delivery.

What is an induced birth?

An induced labour and birth is one that is started artificially because there is a risk to your or your baby's health. It can be necessary, for example, because your waters have broken and after 24 hours labour hasn't begun, you are overdue and going over 42 weeks gestation, you have pre-eclampsia or you are 38 weeks pregnant and have gestational diabetes.

Inducing birth frequently alters a woman's labour and birth experience as it can cause very powerful and urgent contractions. Discuss the pros and cons of each method with your midwife or birth team. Induction should only be done as a medical necessity. It shouldn't be requested to fit around holidays, your partner's annual leave, or your preferred obstetrician's availability or because you are fed up with being pregnant.

Your midwife may discuss your 'Bishop's score' as a way of assessing the readiness of your body to respond to induction. The score looks at things like the position of your baby's head, and the position and ripeness of your cervix. If your score is below six out of ten that equates to an 'unripe' cervix and 15 percent of inductions of this type will not progress to labour. Labour can be induced in several ways.

Induced labours are statistically more likely to end up needing assisted delivery such a forceps or ventouse delivery, but it is hard to know if this due to the induction itself or because labours that require induction are themselves more likely to need assistance at both the beginning of labour and the safe delivery of the baby or babies.

Induction by sweep Usually the first attempt at inducing labour is what's called a sweep, and might be suggested from 41 weeks if you are overdue. The midwife inserts her fingers into your vagina and if the cervix is already dilated she will gently separate the membranes (the amniotic sac) from the cervix. If the cervix isn't dilated she may gently massage and open the cervix instead. Sometimes women have around three sweeps. If you have been asked to come in for a sweep and find it uncomfortable or you are not sure what the midwife is doing, do ask her to explain it to you.

Use of prostaglandin gel A common method is to put prostaglandin gel into the vagina to stimulate the cervix to soften and open. Once the gel has been inserted you will be asked to lie down to give the gel a chance to stay in contact with the cervix. You may then go home as it may take around six hours for labour to begin.

Rupturing the membranes If the prostaglandin gel doesn't work, your midwife may discuss the option of artificial rupture of the membranes (ARM) of the amniotic sac. This involves inserting a plastic pointed 'needle' up the vagina and through the cervix to perforate or cut a hole in the membranes. ARM works better if the cervix is already softening and effacing and can be uncomfortable so pregnant women are offered gas and air to help them to cope with the procedure.

There is a danger of infection once the membranes are ruptured as the sac keeps out microbes in the birth canal. For this reason, ARM isn't used in isolation and is generally only recommended when early labour has been established.

Intravenous syntocinon Induction involves having a canula fitted on your arm. The canula has a tube attached to allow intravenous fluids containing syntocinon to be added into your bloodstream. Syntocinon is an artificial form of oxytocin, the hormone produced by the pituitary gland at the end of pregnancy that causes the uterus to contract.

If the syntocinon is effective, your contractions are likely to be stronger, more frequent and more painful than natural contractions. As you are on a drip you will also be less mobile, which can make it harder to get into active birthing positions that can help you cope with the contractions. In addition, you will need also continuous monitoring with an EFM (see page 108), which makes moving around doubly difficult. As a result women are more likely to ask for an epidural.

Will I need more pain relief in induced birth?

Even if your original birth plan was to have no artificial pain relief (beyond gas and air) you should bear in mind that induced labours are often much more intense that a 'normal' labour. You may want to discuss pain-relief options, especially if you can no longer have a water birth or be really mobile (which both are effective ways of managing labour pains) and may be separated from your birthing partner until you are in active labour and can go to a delivery room. Some hospitals are looking into letting birth partners stay with induced women throughout so ask if this is possible for you.

What is a Caesarean section?

When there are difficulties in pregnancy a decision may be made to deliver your baby surgically by Caesarean section. This can be a planned procedure (generally before your due date), or the need can arise during labour, in which case it will be done as an emergency. Most planned Caesareans use an epidural or full spinal block for pain relief so you are awake throughout and will be able to breastfeed and care for your baby straightaway, providing he does not need urgent medical attention. Caesarean sections take place in theatre. There will a large medical team present including:

- obstetrician who does the surgery
- obstetrician acting as surgical assistant
- midwife
- anaesthetist (who administers the epidural or spinal block)
- anaesthetic nurse
- scrub nurse
- theatre nurses
- birth partner

If your baby may need care after the delivery you may also have a paediatric team present to focus on the baby.

How long will the operation be?

Before surgery you will have a catheter inserted so urine can pass without you needing to go to the loo. You will lie on your side on the operating table, while the anaesthetist puts a needle into the space between your vertebrae and blocks all pain from the chest down. He or she will check this by dripping water on your tummy to demonstrate that you can't feel it. A screen will usually be put in front of your head so you can't see the surgeons.

A straightforward Caesarean takes about an hour. The baby is usually delivered in the first ten minutes, once the surgeon has made an incision in your abdomen and uterus. This incision is usually lateral across the top of your pubic hairline. You will have been asked to shave the top of your pubic hair if it is a planned procedure; the team will shave you if it's an emergency. The rest of the time is taken up by delivery of the placenta and then stitching up the incisions.

As your baby is delivered you can feel yourself being moved from side to side and will be aware of a sensation in your abdomen. It's not at all painful but a bit like someone is 'washing up' in your tummy. As soon as your baby is born, if all is well, he can be placed on your chest for skin-to-skin contact, but it's not too easy lying on your back so you might ask for your head and shoulders to be raised a little so you can cuddle your baby while the surgeon sews up the incisions.

After the surgery is over you will be taken to a recovery room. You baby can stay with you unless he needs special baby care (see page 134). In this case he be taken straight to the baby unit; your birth partner can go with him if you want. After about two hours you will be transferred to the postnatal ward where you will stay for two or three days with your baby to recover.

What happens if it's an emergency Caesarean?

If your baby is getting distressed, or your or your baby's health is at risk the decision might be made to deliver the baby by an emergency Caesarean. If you are in labour and have already had an epidural this can be topped up, or if there is time, a spinal block can be given. However, in extreme emergencies (which is rare) women may be given a general anaesthetic and will only be roused after their baby is born and the surgery is over.

What is a natural Caesarean section?

Natural Caesareans were developed at Queen Charlotte's and Chelsea Hospital in London. The idea was to try and make a Caesarean birth as similar to a natural delivery as possible by slowing down the delivery of the baby, delaying the cutting of the cord and allowing the mum and baby to be in close skin-to-skin contact after the birth. This is a birth where the focus is on the experience of the baby and the mother rather than viewing a Caesarean simply as a surgical procedure.

Natural Caesareans are not widely available in the UK but it is worth talking to your antenatal team if you would like to explore the possibility of having one at a different hospital or your obstetricians may be able to incorporate some of the parts of the procedure into your Caesarean delivery.

How is a natural Caesarean different?

Unlike in a standard Caesarean delivery, the barrier is lowered so that you can both see your baby being born and discover the sex of the baby yourselves. The area is kept sterile in the same way but the baby is delivered more slowly: the obstetrician lifts out one shoulder and then another, slowly easing the baby out and fluid is squeezed out of the baby's lungs as it is born.

The cord is usually cut very quickly in a Caesarean section but during a natural caesarean the cutting of the cord is delayed (see page 144). NICE guidelines recommend delaying the cutting of the cord to allow all the fetal blood to move across into the baby's body, which is important for oxygenation and iron stores and is what happens in nature.

All the assessments of the baby by the midwife and any injections – for example, Vitamin K can be done while the baby is skin-to-skin contact with the mum. The baby can be weighed while the mum is gently moved off the operating table onto a bed and taken to the recovery room. At this time the birth partner can also hold and cuddle the baby.

Mums who previously had a tough birth and even postnatal depression have reported that a gentle mother-centred Caesarean birth was wonderful and a healing experience. The difference in the surgical technique is small, but the experience is much better for mums and dads and probably more gentle for the baby too.

Can I be injured during birth?

Birth injuries range from stretching, bruising and tears to – in rare cases – severe tears and fractures. In addition, women can develop medical conditions brought on by pregnancy such as pre-eclampsia (see page 66) or gestational diabetes (see page 64). If midwives and obstetricians attending a birth are concerned about potential injury to the mum or danger to the baby, they will discuss with the option of intervening to assist your delivery.

The subject of birth injury and birth trauma is rarely talked about. Some people are embarrassed to discuss it, or they don't want to put other women off. But it's good to talk about it since there are some things you can do to reduce your chances of injury, although sometimes it's just a case of bad luck and there would have been nothing you could have done to prevent it. This section is not designed to scare you but rather to inform you and give you more of an idea of how to get help if it happens to you.

What is the risk of physical injury?

You may sustain physical injury during delivery of a baby. You are at higher risk if you have: a big baby (especially over 4 kg/9 lb), a rapid second stage of labour, torn in a previous delivery; had a forceps or ventouse delivery; a baby in an abnormal birth presentation, such as breech or sideways.

Placental abruption This is a very serious condition where the placenta separates fully or partially from the blood supply provided by the uterus. This causes internal blood loss in the mother and means that the placenta is not able to deliver oxygen and nutrients to the baby. This occurs in less than two percent of women, but can result in premature birth, stillbirth or even death of the baby shortly after birth. Around 80 percent of placental abruptions are accompanied by bleeding so get urgent assessment of your baby and placenta if you bleed. Other symptoms include broken waters containing blood, reduced movement in the baby, abdominal pain and continual contracting of the uterus.

Episiotomy When the baby needs to come out quickly, doctors will perform a cut (called an episiotomy) if they think the mother will tear badly without it. If this isn't performed, the mother might suffer serious tears. Episiotomy may also need to be performed for forceps or ventouse deliveries (see page 116-117).

Tears Sometimes if the baby is born very quickly the vaginal area can tear. Tears are described as first-degree tears (quite common little tears that do not need suturing), second-degrees, third-degree and even fourth-degree tears (this is where there is a tear through to the anus and muscle tissue is damaged). Some tears can involve several layers of tissue and will need stitching. Around three to four percent of women who give birth vaginally will suffer third- and fourth-degree tears that require surgery. New guidelines being discussed by obstetricians would assess labouring women for risk of tearing. The theory is, the thicker the perineum (the distance from vagina to anus), the less likely the area is to tear. Conversely, thinner perineums are more likely to tear, so an obstetrician may help to reduce bad tearing in more 'at risk' women. Other risk factors for tearing include big babies, shoulder presentation, rapid second stage of labour and those who have suffered a tear in a previous birth.

Obstetric fistula An obstetric fistula is a hole between rectal and vaginal passages that can sometimes result from a difficult birth. This will need to be repaired with surgery after the delivery.

Suturing After an episiotomy or some tears during birth, or a Caesarean, a mother will require stitching. These stitches can sometimes become infected or open slightly.

Nerve damage Nerves around the vaginal and rectal area can be damaged during a difficult birth. Sometimes the nerve damage will recover, but the damage can be permanent.

Stretching and bruising of muscles Stretching of the pelvic muscles during birth can cause incontinence. Bruising and swelling can make going to the toilet (and sitting down) painful, and bladder control difficult. Treatment can include pelvic floor exercises and in some cases surgery may be required to treat resulting incontinence.

What is the likelihood of psychological damage?
Women giving birth can end up with post-traumatic stress disorder (PTSD) or birth trauma from an experience involving the threat of death or serious injury to themselves or their baby. The reasons why some women experience birth trauma can include:

- feelings of loss of control and extreme vulnerability
- upsetting attitudes of the people attending the birth
- absence of informed consent to medical procedures
- exhaustion from lengthy labour
- poor pain relief
- fear for the baby's safety or a mother's own safety
- birth of a damaged baby
- previous trauma revisited (for example, childhood trauma or domestic violence)

If you are injured in any way during your birth, the most important thing is to talk to your doctor or midwife straight away. They will be able to give you the help you need. Remember, if something has happened to you, it has probably happened to a lot of other people as well, and there will be support out there for you. Many maternity hospitals offer an afterthoughts service where a midwife or obstetrician will go through your labour notes with you and discuss the birth, reasons behind decisions made and how you felt during the process. This can really help mums to feel acceptance and understanding and forgiveness of what happened during the birth of their baby.

If you have had a difficult or traumatic birth you may need to recover before spending time with your baby. If your baby has to be taken straight to the neonatal intensive care unit (NICU) or the special care baby unit (SCBU), see if your partner can be with your baby while you are in recovery. Even after a straightforward Caesarean delivery, you will have to remain in a recovery ward for two hours before you can see your baby (if she needs special care and can't stay with you). You can also ask your partner to give your baby a clean handkerchief or muslin that has been next to your skin so that she knows your smell. The hospital staff will make it a priority that you are taken to your baby as soon as medically possible. In the meantime they will bring you a photo of your baby safe in the NICU. They may also help you to express some colostrum so that your baby can receive a first feed of your milk. Ask for all this to happen if it isn't offered automatically.

When you are reunited with your baby, lay her on your chest in skin-to-skin contact if you can. This so-called 'kangaroo care' is really beneficial to both of you (see page 137). The more time you can spend cuddling, smelling, feeding and talking to your baby, the sooner you will begin to feel like a mum to this new baby.

If you feel very sad and overwhelmed in the days after your baby is born, talk to the hospital staff, your doctor, your health visitor or your community midwife if you are already home. They will be able to advise you about local support and help you to bond with your baby. Even if you are depressed it will really help you both to have lots of skin-to-skin and eye contact. It will also calm your baby, reduce crying and make it easier to be together. Your new baby has no expectations and will unconditionally love you, accept you and want to be with you.

Chapter 6: The early hours and days

Your newborn baby is completely reliant on you – unlike, say, a newborn foal, which struggles to its feet soon after birth. A newborn human is uniquely vulnerable. Your baby will require you to do everything for her – to carry her, feed her and keep her safe and clean. She won't even start to try to walk until she's nearly a whole year old. During her first year, the neurons in her brain will make millions and millions of connections. In this year, more than any other in her whole life, she will absorb more and learn more than she ever will again. The amount of love and care you give her during this time is of huge importance. Science shows clearly now that this foundation will impact on her ability to become a happy, independent and resilient adult.

What is the fourth trimester?

The fourth trimester describes a baby's first 12 weeks, or three months, of life – it's a period of attachment. Your baby is learning about you, and you are learning about him. Attachment parenting experts recommend that babies are carried most of the time and fed on demand, as they were in the womb.

How will I bond with my baby?

Bonding is not necessarily something that will happen straight away. In films and television dramas, it happens the instant the perfect clean baby is placed on the beautiful mother's chest and everyone cries with happiness. In real life it can be a much slower than that. The important thing to remember is that it's OK and it's normal. There are things worth understanding so that you know how to encourage bonding. Putting your baby on your chest as soon as he is born really helps. Lots of skin-to-skin contact everyday and night also helps – skin-to-skin contact promotes the release of the bonding hormone, oxytocin. Breastfeeding also releases oxytocin. See our tips on helping bonding if you're bottle-feeding as well – you needn't miss out. It's like a feedback loop – the more you do (even if you don't yet feel the bond) to promote oxytocin, the more it will build up and then the feelings of attachment and love will start to flow. Then you'll find it will probably spiral upwards. Always seek guidance if you're concerned things don't feel right – your midwife, health visitor or family will know what to do, and it's definitely not an uncommon issue.

How does skin-to-skin contact help?
Skin-to-skin contact with your baby provides several benefits to you and your baby that have been reported in medical studies. It helps you bond and it can:

- regulate your baby's body temperature and breathing
- calm your baby
- allow a gentle transition for your baby from womb to world
- colonise your baby's skin and gut with your own friendly skin flora
- stimulate breastfeeding behaviour in your baby; he will 'crawl' with arms and legs, rooting for your nipple and breast
- recognise your smell and the smell of your milk

Is my baby checked at birth?
Yes, your baby will have what's called an Apgar test immediately after her birth (see box on the next page) then she will be weighed and measured (length and head circumference), and the midwife will check her heart and lungs, spine, hips, as will a paediatrician before you are both discharged from hospital (see page 131). If you have a home birth, the midwife will do all these checks.

WHAT IS THE APGAR TEST?

The Apgar scale was developed by Dr Virginia Apgar in the 1950s. Since that time it has been used internationally to quickly assess babies straight after they are born. It helps the midwife or medical team decide if a baby needs any special care after birth. When your baby is born your baby will be assessed at 0 minutes and 5 minutes and given a score of 0, 1 or 2 for each of the following characteristics:

Appearance – **P**ulse – **G**rimace – **A**ctivity – **R**espiration

Appearance
0 = blue/pale all over
1 = blue at extremities
2 = pink

Pulse
0 = no pulse
1 = fewer than 100 beats per minute
2 = more than 100 beats per minute

Grimace (Irritability to response)
0 = no response
1 = grimace or feeble cry to pain stimulus
2 = cry or pull away from pain stimulus

Activity
0 = none, floppy
1 = some flexing of limbs
2 = flexed arms and legs that offer resistance

Respiration
0 = no breathing
1 = weak, gasping or irregular breathing
2 = strong, loud cry

What does the score show?

Most newborn babies who are given a score above 7 need no further treatment. An Apgar Score of 5-7 may lead to help with breathing such as oxygen or vigorously rubbing the baby's body. If a baby had a score below 5 after five minutes, a paediatrician would be called. The baby would be placed into the hot cot or resuscitaire trolley that is in every delivery room and be given oxygen, or in extreme cases, emergency first aid to encourage him to breathe.

A low score does not necessarily mean that your baby has a long-term problem. It is likely to be lower if you have had a complicated birth, have given birth prematurely, or even had pethidine during labour. The score is used to identify which babies need the extra help straightaway.

What does a newborn baby look like?

You newborn baby will probably have a big head, no visible neck, a big body, but tiny bottom, arms and legs. He might have a pointy head from coming through your birth canal. His skull will have soft spots on it – known as fontanelles. His hands and feet may be a little blue at first as well. He may be bald, or have a surprising amount of hair. If he's Caucasian his eyes will probably be dark blue – a baby's 'true' eye colour develops much later. Most babies of African or Asian descent have dark-grey or brown eyes. He will be covered with a greasy white goo known as vernix – and premature babies will have this too, probably along with fine downy body hair called lanugo.

What can a baby do at first?

When your baby is born he will display the following inbuilt involuntary actions, known as reflexes. Before your baby is discharged from hospital a paediatrician will check many of these reflexes as sometimes their absence can be a sign of neurological damage.

These reflexes will start to disappear over time as your baby develops increased control of his body.

- **Rooting reflex** Your new baby will instinctively turn his head towards your breast (or finger or cheek), with his mouth open wide and ready to latch on to feed. Over time this becomes more voluntary.
- **Suck reflex** If your nipple and breast touches the roof of your baby's mouth he is able to stimulate, suck and massage your breast with his tongue and will automatically swallow each time his mouth fills with milk.
- **Moro reflex** If your baby experiences a loss of physical support, quick movement or rapid descent, he will extend his limbs, arch his back and then quickly bring in all his limbs (and usually cry) – this is called the Moro reflex. Some scientists have suggested that it might be a reaction that would have helped our ancestor's babies to hang on to their mum when being carried around. Your baby will have lost this reflex completely by the time he is around six months old.
- **Startle reflex** Triggered by loud noises, this is like the Moro reflex but the baby does not fling his arms out and it may serve to protect the back of the neck. Although all humans startle and blink, this involuntary startle reflex is lost by around six months old.
- **Stepping reflex** At birth your baby will making walking movements even though he is unable to bear weight. Before your baby is discharged from hospital a paediatrician may test this reflex by holding him bolt upright with his feet on the hospital bed.
- **Grasp reflex** A beloved reflex as your newborn will automatically grip your finger if you touch the palm of his hand. By the age of four months the reflex begins to disappear and your baby will begin voluntarily grasping objects.
- **Babinski's reflex** If the sole of your baby's foot is stroked from heel to toe it should turn in with the toes arching up – this is the Babinski reflex and he will have lost it by his second birthday. Again it is hypothesised that it may be an ancient protective reflex that prevented babies from falling.

- **Tonic neck reflex** This is a reflex that starts at around four weeks and will have disappeared by the time the baby is six months old. Doctors use the tonic neck reflex to assess your baby. The doctor will lay your baby on his back, then gently turn his head to one side; the arms and legs on the side he is facing should extend while the opposite arm and leg will bend.
- **Dive and swimming reflexes** The dive reflex or 'bradycardic response' occurs in water. When babies are gently brought underwater they hold their breath and open their eyes as a reflex. A Swedish study of the reflex reported that none of the babies inhaled water or choked when they were underwater. This reflex is commonly seen in newborns at swimming lessons, but never assume that a baby can swim as he can't lift his face out of the water.

How far can a newborn baby see?
Your newborn baby can see things around 30 cm (12 in) away quite sharply. Further than that everything will be blurry. It's no coincidence that this is the distance to your face when he is breastfeeding.

Can my baby hear?
Yes, he should be able to. Your baby will probably have his hearing checked soon after birth, generally before you leave hospital. The test is simple and will pick up some hearing defects straight away.

Why is my baby's first poo so dark?
Your baby should poo within 48 hours of being born. The first poo is called meconium and is not digested milk, but the contents of his gut from when he was in the womb (mucus, amniotic fluid, and everything your baby has swallowed while he was in the womb). Meconium is sticky and dark in colour and quite difficult to clean off his bottom. It's important to see the meconium as it's a good sign your baby's gut is moving and working. After a few days your baby's poo will get lighter in colour as all the meconium comes out and is replaced with digested milk. If you are breastfeeding he will produce a mustard-yellow poo with a seed-like consistency. If you are formula-feeding your baby the poo will become a darker brown colour, more like peanut butter. If you

are concerned about your baby's poo; if it contains blood, mucus, is white in colour speak to your midwife or doctor. Bright-green poo can be associated with indigestion and if you are breastfeeding you might want to check that your baby is latched on well. Speak to your midwife or health visitor.

What happens if my baby is unwell at birth?

Nearly 13 percent of newborn babies will need some medical care after birth. Sometimes doctors and parents will already know this because of a pre-existing condition that has been picked up on scans. A seriously ill baby will need to be taken the neonatal intensive care unit (NICU). A baby that needs slightly less intensive medical care would be moved to the special care baby unit (SCBU). Your baby might need special medical care if he was:

- born premature (babies can now survive from 23 weeks gestation, but if they are born before 34 weeks they may need support with breathing, feeding and regulating their temperature initially)
- born small and with low birth weight (also known as 'small for dates' or Inter-uterine growth retardation); these babies may need help with feeding as their bodies diverted energy to their developing brain and their gut may be immature
- born with a pre-existing condition that may need surgery, for example, a heart condition
- born with an infection, such as group B strep
- born to a mother who developed gestational diabetes
- shown to have poor Apgar scores at five minutes
- 'grunting' or experiencing difficulty breathing after the birth
- born after a difficult birth
- born with jaundice, or developed it later

What is neonatal intensive care unit?

Neonatal Intensive Care Unit (NICU), provides special incubators, or temperature-controlled 'hot cots' to keep babies warm and help protect them from infection. Incubators are fitted with respirators that help some poorly or very small babies to breathe and drips that deliver food, such as glucose, and fluids intravenously, via a canula and a tube directly into a baby's bloodstream.

Most babies in the NICU will need help with feeding but not always intravenously; instead they have a little tube up their nose that leads down to the stomach. This means that nurses or parents can give them a feed of the mum's breastmilk, donor milk or formula milk for premature or sick babies.

There will be a very strict cleanliness policy and if you are able to cuddle, feed or change your baby you will need to wash your hands thoroughly with antibacterial cleanser as these babies are very susceptible to infection.

Your baby will be surrounded by monitors and tubes which can be frightening for parents at first.

What is the special care baby unit?

Also known as SCBU, this is a less-intense form of care for babies that need less medical support and the hygiene rules are slightly less rigorous (but you will still need to observe good clean hygiene especially around feeding your baby). Instead of incubators there are usually specialist beds like hot cots and babies are supported with not all but some of the following:

- monitoring of activity, breathing and heart rate
- oxygen
- tube feeding
- phototherapy for jaundice
- establishing breastfeeding and breastmilk expressing

If your baby was in the NICU he will be transferred to the SCUBU as he gets stronger and more independent. This can worry parents as it seems a lot less 'medical', but rest reassured babies are only transferred to the SCUBU when they no longer need intensive care; if the unit was overcrowded, they would have been transferred another hospital neonatal unit). So try to feel confident and enjoy this sign that your baby is getting better.

How can I cope when my baby is on a special ward?

It is very upsetting and stressful if you have to be separated from your baby while she is looked after in neonatal or special care. This is made even more difficult if you are unwell, and recovering from an emergency Caesarean, for example. You may need some help getting to see your baby and recovering at the same time. The good news about being in hospital is that you can quickly be taken to your baby, even at night-time, for feeds and cuddles. The best way for you both to recover is for you to spend as much time as possible with your new baby, with lots of skin-to-skin contact, cuddling and feeding.

If you have been discharged from the postnatal ward and are breastfeeding your baby or expressing and establishing breastfeeding you can ask if your hospital has family rooms so you can sleep on site as night feeding and expressing are very important for both you and your baby to get breastfeeding and milk production going.

If your baby needs surgery you will also have the added stress of waiting while she is in theatre and then helping her to recover afterwards. We recommend that you contact a support group like Bliss or Tommy's as they can help you understand your baby's particular treatment as well as connecting with other parents in your position. You will also probably make strong connections with other parents on the ward who are going through similar difficulties. This can be a real help, but it can also be tough, especially if you learn that another baby there is critically ill.

If you have had a difficult birth and are in recovery, you may not be able to get to your baby. It can be reassuring to have your partner go with your baby and have skin-to-skin contact with her while you are in recovery. If your baby is too ill, he may not be able to cuddle the baby but he can talk to her and may be allowed to put clean muslin cloth that has been next to your skin in the cot so that your baby can smell you. The hospital staff will make sure that you are reunited with your baby as soon as medically possible. In the meantime they will bring you a photo of your baby safe in the NICU.

How can I help my baby in special care?

New mums can feel really frightened and useless if their baby is taken to special baby care and seems to be being looked after by lots of 'strangers.' However, you are your baby's mum and there are lots of things you can do to help your baby that the medical staff are unable to do.

What is kangaroo care?

As soon as the medical staff let you, lay your baby on your chest in skin-to-skin contact; this is known as kangaroo care. Your baby will be placed on your chest like a little tree frog and you can feel him there, smell him and talk to him. There are lots of benefits for newborn babies. It helps to relax and calm them and help with their transition from the womb to the outside world. Skin-to-skin contact regulates a baby's body temperature and can also stimulate your baby to feed, which will in turn stimulate your milk production and your bonding hormone, oxytocin. Finally, there is more and more evidence that babies benefit from lying on their mum's skin so that their skin can be colonised with your 'friendly' skin flora (bacteria). The more time you can spend cuddling, smelling, feeding and talking to your baby, the sooner you will begin to feel like a mum to this new baby.

What should I feed my baby?

Colostrum Express some colostrum so that your baby can receive a first feed. Your colostrum is packed with the perfect fuel for your baby to grow stronger and it even coats the lining of his gut to protect it from infection.

Breastmilk This is really important for babies in special care. However, as babies in special care are often not able to feed effectively, mums are encouraged to start by expressing breastmilk to really get their production going. Most units have fantastic electric pumps, which will allow you to express your breastmilk quickly (from both breasts at the same time) and quietly throughout the day and night. The milk you express can either be fed to your baby immediately or stored for later use. The nurses and midwives will help get you so don't worry if you are only producing a few drops at first. Initially your expressed milk will be given to your baby as a tube feed or a cup feed, you will be able to breastfeed when he is stronger; many premature or poorly babies master breastfeeding quite quickly. Your baby may start with a mixture of breastfeeds, tube feeds, syringe feeds and cup feeds during the day.

Donor or formula milk If there is no donor breast milk available, your baby may need to be given some milk especially formulated for premature babies until you are able to provide all the milk he needs. Again in the early days these feeds will be given via a tube, cup or a bottle if you choose to bottle feed your baby.

Tube feeding If your baby is born premature or unwell he may lack a strong sucking reflex, which may mean he tires easily during feeds. So he will have a little tube that goes up his nose and into his food pipe (oesophagus) so that milk can be given directly to his stomach using gravity and bypassing the mouth (so no choking). You will be shown how to tube feed your baby. It can be a bit scary at first but you'll get the hang of it.

What are the implications of premature birth?

If your baby needs to be born early or is likely to arrive early (the average delivery of twins is 37 weeks and 33 weeks for triplets), you may be admitted as an antenatal patient to a hospital with a NICU – which may not be the original hospital you chose. You may be admitted too if your baby has inter-uterine growth retardation and needs to be delivered when the placenta starts to fail (this is carefully monitored to allow the baby to stay in the uterus for as long as is safe). If you begin having contractions prematurely you may be admitted and given tocolytic drugs in attempt to halt your contractions so that you can have steroid injections. The steroids help mature a premature baby's lungs so they produce the surfactant needed to allow the lungs to function properly, but they take about 24 hours to have any effect.

What are the long-term effects of prematurity?

Some premature babies (by no means all) may need physiotherapy to help promote their muscle tone and strength. The physiotherapist will show you some simple exercises that you help your baby with. A smaller minority of premature babies may begin life with a disability, but again this may not be lifelong.

Will my baby's development be delayed?

Premature babies are actually younger than their full-term counterparts and so they will tend to do things a little later than their birth date would indicate but maybe earlier than their expected due date would predict. Remember to bear this in mind but it's still important to keep an eye on your premature baby's development as early intervention in developmental delay can make a huge difference to your baby's prognosis and development.

Many low-birthweight babies, including premature babies, are offered additional check-ups and are included in research studies that assess their development. It's worth taking your baby along. They may also be offered extra vaccinations as they get older.

Will my baby grow at the same rate if she's premature?

Of course premature babies are smaller than their full-term peers and it takes them a while to catch up in size. They may always be lighter and shorter than some of their peers. When your baby is discharged from hospital you will be advised on nutrition and told whether she needs follow-up appointments. Breastfeeding is particularly important for premature babies as they have immature guts and immune systems and breastmilk provides optimal nutrition (see page 137).

Your baby's health team will check your baby's weight, head circumference and length regularly to see that all these measurements track along her personal growth trajectory. Steady growth is more important than moving to a higher centile for weight and height; in fact, there is some evidence that rapid weight gain can have long-term health consequences.

How quickly will I recover from the birth?

Even if you've had a straightforward birth you can feel like your body isn't back to 'normal' after the birth of your baby. Expect it to take some time (depending on how your birth went) to recover.

Pregnancy, birth and an assisted delivery can leave you with various aches, pains and changes in your body. Some of these are temporary, but may require treatment and others may be permanent: for example, some women will go up a shoe size after their baby is born.

Why are my feet more swollen?

Some women can feel very swollen after the birth. Swelling (oedema) is totally normal. Any fluids resorbed by your uterus, as well as any intravenous fluids received during labour, can gather in your feet and your hands. The swelling should go down within a fortnight. Sometimes your shoe size will go up temporarily or permanently after birth as your ligaments relaxed so your feet may spread.

Why am I leaking urine?

Incontinence after birth is normal and usually temporary. The muscles of the vagina have been stretched during birth and you may find that you leak urine, especially if you laugh or cough unexpectedly. Your vagina will look different following the birth but should recover fairly quickly.

If you are experiencing a lot of leaking, wear a thicker sanitary towel – you'll be wearing one anyway to soak up the bleeding called lochia after birth (see below). Go to the toilet frequently even if you don't feel you need a wee. Tell your doctor at your six-week check if it persists.

If it's just a case of muscle tone you can strengthen your pelvic floor muscles with the kegel or pelvic floor exercises you were taught at your antenatal class (see page 78). They are often included in postnatal yoga and Pilates classes that focus on building core strength after birth.

My breasts feel full already, is this normal?

Usually around three days after the birth, your breasts will swell and feel very full and heavy. This is a sign that your milk has come in. If your breasts become hard and painful they are engorged (which is not the same as your milk coming in) and you need to make sure that your baby is latching on properly and breastfeeding efficiently. Talk to your midwife, or ask her to help you make sure your baby is feeding properly. Once your baby is emptying your breast of milk during a breastfeed the engorgement should pass. If your baby is unable to breastfeed, for example because he is in special care, express milk to ease engorgement and get milk production going.

How long will I have vaginal discharge after the birth?

Postpartum discharge, known as lochia, is blood and cells from the lining of your uterus. This can go on for several weeks and will lighten gradually. It is better to use a thick sanitary pad rather than a tampon, which carries a risk of infection. You may feel afterpains, which is a sign that your uterus is contracting back to its pre-pregnancy size.

While some blood loss is normal after birth there are some symptoms that need medical attention from your midwife or doctor. If your bleeding is very heavy and bright red, this might be a postpartum haemorrhage; call an ambulance as you need emergency treatment. This may happen within 24 hours of birth (although secondary haemorrhages can occur up to three months after birth). It can result from a retained placenta or the uterus not contracting back to its pre-pregnancy size. Call your midwife or doctor straight away if your blood loss or lochia has an unpleasant smell, you feel feverish, bleeding stays bright red after 7 days, or your abdomen feels tender. Emergency symptoms accompanied by the blood loss include:

- increasingly bright-red blood (especially if this is four days or more since the birth)
- using more than a pad each hour
- blood contains clots bigger than a milk-bottle top
- you feel faint and your heartbeat seems fast or irregular

Will I suffer any hair loss?

During your pregnancy your hair may have been your crowning glory as you don't suffer from normal hair loss. However, after your baby is born your oestrogen levels fall, so all this retained hair will start to fall out. This can be noticeable when your baby is about 12 weeks old, but rest assured your hair should return to pre-pregnancy condition in time.

My pelvic floor feels loose and my perineum is sore. Is this normal?
The uterus, bladder and rectum can all fall a bit as a result of labour and birth. Usually this is temporary. Kegel exercises can help strengthen the pelvic floor muscles.

Most women will tear a little bit during birth and about two-thirds of these injuries need a few stitches. Severe third-degree tears are rare, but can affect the muscles around the anus, and will need stitching by the obstetric surgeon. Tears and stitches can feel sore after birth and you can feel like your whole vaginal area is bruised.

To ease the pain of stitches and tears and aid recovery make sure you have a bath each day followed by about five to ten minutes with a bare bottom to give the wound air. If it's very painful a cold gel pack can ease the swelling and the pain. You can rent a 'valley' cushion from the NCT. It looks like a donut and allows you to keep the pressure off the wound when you sit down.

The first time you have a poo after birth can be stressful. Eat plenty of fruit and vegetables, and drink lots of water so you avoid straining with constipation.

Why have I developed piles?
Piles, or haemorrhoids, are swollen blood vessels in the rectum. They are common in pregnancy and women also develop them after birth from the huge pressure of pushing. They can be very itchy, sore and uncomfortable. Again, cold gel packs can relieve the discomfort but speak to your doctor if they haven't gone by the time you have your six-week check. You should keep the area clean and patted dry and you can gently push the piles back inside while you are in the shower. If you use a cream make sure that it is suitable for breastfeeding women.

How much can I do after a Caesarean delivery?

It can be a shock to try and sit up after you've had a Caesarean as the muscles you use to sit up have been cut to deliver your baby. It's important to get up and about as soon as you can after the birth, but it's normal to feel a little shaky the first time you wee, poo or have a shower. At first you will need to gently support your scar when you go to the loo or feel a sneeze coming on as it will hurt. You may also suffer with trapped wind caused by air getting into your abdomen during the surgery. Some wards will give you a drink of warm water with peppermint oil, which can help to ease the discomfort.

Once the dressing has been removed (usually in the shower), you will need to keep the scar clean and dry (after showers) and look out for redness, puss or signs of infection. Depending on the kind of stitches or staples your surgeon used they may need to removed after about a week; your midwife can do this when you are back at home.

A Caesarean section is major abdominal surgery so be gentle with yourself after the birth. Rest as much as you can. No heavy lifting or hoovering and don't go up and down stairs too much. Check your car insurance as you may not be able to drive for a few weeks.

Postnatal Pilates and yoga can help rebuild your core muscle strength, which is particularly helpful after a Caesarean.

What will happen if my birth doesn't go as planned or I feel depressed or traumatised?

If you have had a difficult, upsetting or traumatic birth you may need time to recover physically and mentally regroup before focusing on your baby. But it can be more difficult if you are physically separated from your baby, because you are in an operating theatre or your baby is transferred to special care. The hospital will reunite you as soon as is possible.

If you cannot walk, your bed may be wheeled into the special baby ward so that you can see, hold or even feed your baby. If you do feel traumatised ask the nurses caring for your baby to let you try 'kangaroo care' (see page 137); it can be very relaxing and calming for both you and your baby.

This can obviously be more difficult if either you or your baby is ill. Don't exhaust yourself and get as much help and support to see your baby as you can. It can also help to know that your birth partner or your mum can spend lots of time cuddling and caring for your baby while you recover.

If you had a very traumatic birth but you can't really remember what happened, talk to your midwife. Many hospitals run 'afterthoughts' sessions where you can go through the notes about labour and birth with a midwife or doctor. This can really help you to understand what happened on the day.

I am feeling depressed. What should I do?

If you feel very sad, angry, frustrated and overwhelmed in the days after your baby is born, speak to the hospital staff, your doctor, midwife or health visitor. They will be able to advise you about local support and help you to bond with your baby. Mums with postnatal depression or high anxiety often feel that their baby 'doesn't love them' or they are not 'good enough' to look after their baby.

Even if you are depressed and exhausted it will really help you and your baby to have lots of skin-to-skin cuddles and make eye contact. This will help to calm your baby, reduce crying and help your establish breastfeeding (if that is what you want and hope to do). Your baby has no expectations and will unconditionally love you, accept you and want to be with you. Babies love to be held, love your voice, love your smell and are content to be near you. Even if they cry they like to be with you.

Keep things simple at this time. You don't need to be the hostess with the most-est and have a string of visitors. Let yourself be looked after, accept help with food and caring for the baby. Try to make sure that you have time to sleep in the day and time for a shower and time for a hot cup of tea in peace. All these bits of self-care will help you to live in the moment and take each day as it comes. Eat well and as you feel stronger try some yoga or swimming.

When can I go home from hospital?

All being well it may be possible to go home a few hours after the birth. If there are any concerns you may stay a day or two. If you've had a Caesarean, provided your baby is well, you will generally be discharged after around three days.

You will be given your hand-held notes to hand over to your community midwife when she does a home visit. You may be given a copy of the letter with details of your baby's birth for your family doctor (although this may be sent direct to your doctor). You will be provided with instructions on how to register your baby's birth, which you are legally required to do before he six weeks old. Before you and your baby can be discharged:

- A hospital paediatrician will check out your baby for any signs of infection, developmental problems or ill health. If all is okay he will be formally discharged.
- An obstetrician or midwife will assess you. She will ask if you've had a wee, examine any stitches and take your temperature. If all is okay you will be formally discharged.
- Your baby will have a routine hearing screening test to rule out hearing impairment.
- You will be offered vitamin K for your baby to help his blood clot properly and to prevent bleeding into the brain. If you consent, your baby will receive an injection or oral dose of vitamin K; if you have it orally then you need to take two more vials of vitamin K home with you. One to be given at one week, the second to be given at one month after birth.
- If you are breastfeeding make sure that you have had support and had a couple of latching-on attempts and feeds before you leave. Help now can really help you to establish breastfeeding and avoid a poor latch and lots of pain and discomfort for you and poor feeds for your baby. This is crucial.

BRINGING HOME A 'SPECIAL BABY CARE' BABY

If your baby has needed special care, then the anxiety and excitement of going home together is even greater, especially if your baby may have been in the special care unit for several weeks. Many parents worry about how they will cope without all the back up they have had over the last few weeks or months.

Try to remember that your baby (or babies) is being discharged because he is ready for life at home. You may still need to have a oxygen on hand or a feeding tube might still be attached so make sure you chat through your baby's extra needs and remember you will have lots of support in the community special baby care team.

Bringing your baby home from hospital

Unless you can push your baby home in a pram or carry him in a baby sling on the bus, you will need a car seat for your baby suitable for a newborn. Before your baby is born have a few goes at practising attaching the car seat. Prepare for a slow and momentous drive home as (especially for dads) this is often when it sinks in that you are utterly responsible for the care of your new baby. Most new mums cannot wait to get home from the busy postnatal ward. Make sure that you have planned and got support lined up from your partner and family as the first days at home can be a tough transition.

Will I get help from the community midwife?

Depending on your hospital trust and whether or not this is your first baby, you should receive a daily visit from your community midwife for about ten days – or in some areas up to 28 days. She will check that your baby is doing well, ask how feeding is going and make sure you are recovering from the birth. She will weigh your baby at each visit to confirm your baby is regaining her birth weight (most babies lose a bit of weight in the first days after the birth). Write down any questions you want to ask before she comes just in case you forget something. Your midwife can help you with:

- latching on properly and establishing breastfeeding
- bottle- and formula-feeding advice, if you choose to bottle-feed.
- everyday care and safety advice such as cord care, bathing and cleaning your baby, nappies and poo questions, sleeping and SIDS advice; ask her if you if you want help with bathing your baby for the first time

When you and your midwife are happy, you will then be discharged from her care and passed over to your community health visitor.

TESTING YOUR BABY FOR SERIOUS ILLNESS – HEEL-PRICK TEST

About five days after the birth, your midwife will do a heel-prick test to test for up to nine serious but rare illnesses, many of which can be improved if treated early. The test includes screening for:

- phenylketonuria (PKU)
- cystic fibrosis
- sickle cell disease
- congenital hypothyroidism
- thyroid hormone deficiency
- medium-chain acyl-CoA dehydrogenase deficiency (MCADD) tested in some babies

If any of the test come back positive you will be contacted by your doctor.

How will I cope at home in the early days?

These first few days and weeks with your baby are all about bonding, getting to know your baby and learning to be a parent. We would recommend that you keep things simple. Stay in your nightclothes if this helps you, and ask family and friends to take over domestic chores. You will quickly exhaust yourself if have to look after lots of guests and get out and about. Stocking up on freezer meals and clean clothes before the baby was born (see page 82) should now leave you time to:

- recover from the birth, both physically and emotionally
- establishing breastfeeding
- get to know your baby with lots of skin-to-skin contact and cuddles, which will help you bond and relax
- catch up on rest and sleep and enjoy your baby

I am feeling overwhelmed. Is this normal?

The 'baby blues' are a very common phenomenon, where new mums feel overwhelmed, tearful and sad. This tends to happen around three to four days after your baby is born and coincides with a huge drop in progesterone levels in your body (much bigger than that observed around pre-menstrual syndrome to give you an idea of the hormonal change you are experiencing).

You will also be tired and still not recovered from the birth so be kind to yourself at this time. Speak to your midwife or health visitor if you start to feel depressed. These feelings are very common in the tough first weeks with your baby. If you think that your depression is more than baby blues, talk to your health visitor or family doctor about postnatal depression.

How does breastfeeding work?

Healthcare professionals around the world and the UK Department of Health agree that it's best to breastfeed your baby exclusively for the first six months, if you can. Breastmilk not only meets all of your baby nutritional needs, but there are a lot of benefits for mum as well.

Breastmilk is the perfect baby food. It contains over 100 ingredients, including important fats (for brain development), proteins, sugars and enzymes. You produce exactly the right amount and it's 'served' at the perfect temperature. Breastmilk also contains hormones and growth factors for optimal growth as well as antibodies to build your baby's immune system. Breastmilk collects in ducts in your breasts and when the baby starts to drink the milk your, breasts make more milk. The more the baby feeds the more you make. Babies who are fed exclusively on breastmilk:

- are significantly less likely to suffer with gastroenteritis, which is a severe tummy upset
- suffer less with chest infections.
- have protection from a strong family history of allergies and eczema which helps avoid developing those problems themselves
- are protected by the colostrum (that you will produce at first) as it will coat the lining of your baby's gut with antibodies, this can really help her immature tummy and protect her from 'necrotising fasciitis', which is a very nasty and potentially life-threatening infection that is a particular danger for premature and poorly babies
- also benefit from a tuned-in mum as the hormones that mums produce when they are breastfeeding seem to really help them to tune in to their baby and produce a fast-track to a very close bond. (The good news is this is that if you are bottle-feeding your baby, you can also feed her in a similar way to help promote the lovely close bond with your baby.)

What is colostrum?
The first kind of milk that your breasts produce is a very special kind of milk called colostrum. It is really concentrated milk and is also full of your antibodies, which helps protect your baby from infections. It's very precious and your breasts only produce very small amounts. Doctors and midwives call it 'liquid gold'.

How much milk does my new baby need?

At birth a baby's stomach is the size of a small marble. It is designed to digest rich colostrum and fills up really quickly (so colostrum is only produced in small amounts). Your baby's stomach can almost completely digest and absorb your colostrum. This efficiency means that her stomach will empty very quickly and this is why newborn babies need frequent feeds.

How does the supply work?

Your milk production works on a supply-and-demand system controlled by your baby's feeding behaviour. When she feeds, your breasts make more milk to replace that feed and more. As tiring as it is, night-time feeding is vital for building up your milk supply in the early days with your baby. Newborn babies can't and should not be expected to sleep through the night. If they did, your breasts would become engorged as the milk produced at night wasn't emptied. Also not feeding would reduce your supply and you would not make enough breastmilk.

What is the let-down reflex?

When your baby sucks at the breast it triggers oxytocin to be produced in your brain, which stimulates a let-down reflex. The muscles in your breast contract, pushing milk down towards the nipple and your baby. The let-down reflex feels different to different mums; some feel tingling or cramping under their armpit or in their breast, others don't feel anything at all – the milk just comes down. In time, just thinking about your baby or hearing him cry can trigger let-down. Oxytocin is the hormone that helped your labour contractions and still does this now to help your uterus to contract to pre-pregnancy size. You will feel these 'after pains' and they will feel like small contractions.

Breastfeeding is hungry and thirsty work

Breastfeeding a baby burns an extra 500 calories a day. This can make you feel hungry, but there is still no need to 'eat for two'. Lots of mums also report feeling desperately thirsty when they begin to breastfeed, so always have a big glass of water to hand when you breastfeed.

Breastfeeding twins and multiples

Nowadays lots of mums who know the benefits of breastmilk choose to breastfeed their twins or multiples. The La Leche League report that it saves mothers of twins both money and time as the time making up and sterilising bottles is even higher with twins and multiples. Breastfeeding mums are generally able to produce enough milk for their twins or multiples due the their bodies' clever supply-and-demand system.

HOW DO I KNOW MY BABY IS GETTING ENOUGH MILK?

Your baby should be getting enough to drink if:

- he appears healthy and alert
- by the third day after birth your baby he is producing about six wet nappies a day
- by the fourth or fifth day (usually before) he produces at least two mustard-yellow poos a day (each dirty nappy at least the size of a two-pound coin)
- your baby is gaining weight after the first two weeks. Don't wait this long if you think your baby is not latched on properly, swallowing and feeding well. Speak to a breastfeeding supporter if you are concerned that your baby isn't feeding well and if feeding is painful, your nipples are sore or your baby is making a clicking sound when breastfeeding.)

If you think your baby is not weeing and or pooing, then it's really urgent that you get help. Call your midwife or health visitor.

What do I need if I want to bottle-feed?

If you're planning to bottle-feed your baby you'll need to buy all the equipment before your baby is born. You will need bottles and newborn teats (at least six of each) and some means of sterilising the equipment (see below), as well as brushes to clean the bottles and teats.

- Anything that comes into contact with milk needs to be sterilised – bottles, teats, bottle covers, spoons even the knife you use to level the formula in the scoop.
- Make up a fresh bottle for every feed.
- Always follow the instructions on the tin – never add extra powder to the feed as this can lead to constipation and overfeeding.
- Unless your baby is having a special premature baby formula milk you will need to choose a 'first milk' for your formula-fed baby.
- If your baby is exclusively formula-fed his poo will look different from breastfed baby poo. It looks more like peanut butter or a brown curry.
- Bottle-fed babies produce more dirty nappies because the formula milk isn't as completely digested as breastmilk. The poo may be a little smellier, which may be due to your baby developing a different gut flora to a breastfed baby.
- Most babies can digest formula milk okay, but a small minority will be allergic to the cow's protein in the formula. Speak to your health visitor if your baby shows signs of an allergy such as a rash or seems very uncomfortable. Don't change his diet without advice.
- Babies with severe reflux are sometimes prescribed heavy, thicker formulas so they don't vomit them up so easily.
- Bottle-feed your baby in the same way as you would breastfeed and try to feed your baby yourself.
- Try to recognise and respect your baby's signals of hunger and fullness.
- Be sure to have lots of eye and skin-to-skin contact to promote bonding.
- Enjoy feeding your baby as your special time together.

Index

Acknowledgements

We would like to thank the following organisations for their guidance and expert advice:

Royal College of Paediatrics and Child Health (RCPCH)
www.rcpch.ac.uk
The RCPCH mission is to transform child health through knowledge, innovation and expertise. The Essential Parent Company provides video clips to the RCPCH. These are used to help train junior paediatricians in the UK and abroad.

UNICEF UK Baby Friendly Initiative
www.unicef.org.uk/babyfriendly/
The UK Baby Friendly Initiative is based on a global accreditation programme of UNICEF and the World Health Organization. It is designed to support breastfeeding and parent/infant relationships by working with public services to improve standards of care.

We would also like to thank the following experts who have generously donated their time and expertise to help expectant and new mums and dads all over the world.

Melissa Little, Paediatric Dietitian and Baby Nutrition Expert
Melissa Little is a practising member of the Freelance Dietician's Group and Paediatric Group and is fully registered with the Health Professionals Council and the British Dietetic Association.

Alison Ross, Registered Midwife, DipHe, BSc (Hons)
Alison Ross is a specialist midwife for mental health at Kingston Hospital. As well as all the practical skills of looking after a new baby, she is specially trained in supporting new mums who are feeling overwhelmed, sad and depressed.

Dr Sarah Temple MBBChir MRCGP DRCOG
www.ehcap.co.uk/dr-sarah-temple
Dr Sarah Temple is The Essential Parent Company's expert children's GP. She is working as a portfolio NHS GP in Somerset. With more than 20 years' experience working with children and young people, both within general practice and mental health services, Sarah has a special interest in the link between child and parental well-being.

Dr Emily Gelson, Registrar in Obstetrics and Gynaecology
Cambridge University Hospital Trust

Personal thanks

Dr Rebecca Chicot
I would like to thank my parents, Katrina and Brian; my siblings, Daniel and Katie; and my own growing family: Rufus, Miranda, Benedict and Iris. Together you have confirmed my belief that the secret of happiness is family and you have helped me in my work at The Essential Parent Company to support new parents and their families. Thanks also to Professor Winston for sharing his huge wealth of wisdom and experience in the fields of fertility, pregnancy and baby development.

Diana Hill
I would like to thank my son, Oscar, for inspiring the creation of The Essential Parent Company. I would also like to thank my husband, Shawn, for his ongoing patience and support and my wonderful parents, Elizabeth and Douglas. Thanks to the 'Bright Birds' for their ideas! Last and not least I would like to thank 'Prof' Robert Winston for being such an inspiring, generous and wonderful mentor and collaborator.

Together, we would like to thank our four extraordinary investors, Robert Clarke, Ralph Kanter, John Spearman and Hyman Bielsky, who have continued to believe in our work over the years. Without their financial, intellectual, creative and emotional support, this project would never have happened. Finally, thanks to Victoria Marshallsay for being such a patient and thoughtful editor.

The Genesis Research Trust

www.genesisresearchtrust.com

Despite countless breakthroughs in medical science, we still do not understand why some pregnancies will end in tragedy. For most of us, having a child of our own is the most fulfilling experience of our lives. All of us can imagine the desperation and sadness of parents who lose a baby, and the life-shattering impact that a disabled or seriously ill child has on a family.

Led by Professor Robert Winston, The Genesis Research Trust raises money for the largest UK-based collection of scientists and clinicians who are researching the causes and cures for conditions that affect the health of women and babies. This trust is uniquely based in the building where the scientists carry out their research at the Wolfson and Weston Research Institute for Family Health, on the Hammersmith Campus of Imperial College London.

The objectives of the trust are to provide financial assistance for medical research and teaching in the field of gynaecology, obstetrics and related fields in paediatrics. The trust is organised in order to promote, by all available means, the study of healthy childbearing and diseases of women. Our teaching programme is internationally recognised and the work produced has the highest reputation among academics and researchers. Our courses and symposia are attended by approximately 3,000 full- and part-time students per year.

Advances in the well-being of women and babies can only be achieved by research into the disorders that can affect anyone. Our primary aim is to improve the health of the unborn child and its mother.

The Essential Parent Company

www.essentialparent.com

If you would like more information about our company and the fertility, pregnancy, birth and online baby-care courses we create, please visit our website.